To: Dad
Merry Christmas

Love: *[signature]*

THE WORLD'S WORST AIRCRAFT

THE WORLD'S WORST AIRCRAFT

Bill Yenne

JG PRESS

ISBN 1-57215-293-1

Acknowledgements

The author wishes to thank the following people who have helped make this book possible: Dean Slaybaugh; Bob Foster of McDonnell Douglas; Captain George Cully of the US Air Force Historical Research Center; MV Brown of British Aerospace; Russell D Egnor of the US Navy; TSgt Barry L Sprink of the US Air Force Office of Air Force History; RAR Wilson of Historical Aviation Service; Carleen Bentley of the Donald Douglas Museum; SR Elliot; Art Krieger; James Gilbert, whose 1975 book by the same title served as an inspiration of sorts; and finally Jim Chandler at BDB, who talked Syd Mayer into undertaking this somewhat unusual project.

Designed by Bill Yenne
Edited by John Kirk

Page 1: The Convair XFY-1 Pogo was first flown in August 1954. Designed for vertical takeoffs, it was virtually impossible to land because the pilot had to look over his shoulder. The landing gear were fine on dry land, but can you imagine these on a slippery carrier deck in high seas?

Pages 2-3: Named for Britain's wartime Aircraft Production Minister Lord Brabazon, the Bristol Model 167 cost British taxpayers 12.5 million pounds. First flown in 1949, the single prototype was overweight, underpowered and never certified to operate above 25,000 feet. Intended as a 100-passenger airliner, it never entered service and was cut up for scrap in 1953.

Below: Walter Barling's huge NBL-1 heavy bomber first flew in August 1923 and could reach 700 feet in 20 minutes. Like many of the aircraft in this book, it was overweight, underpowered and extraordinarily expensive. It was also very short on range. It could fly 335 miles without refuelling, but only if it didn't carry any bombs. To have used it in wartime would have necessitated several refuelling stops *inside* enemy territory.

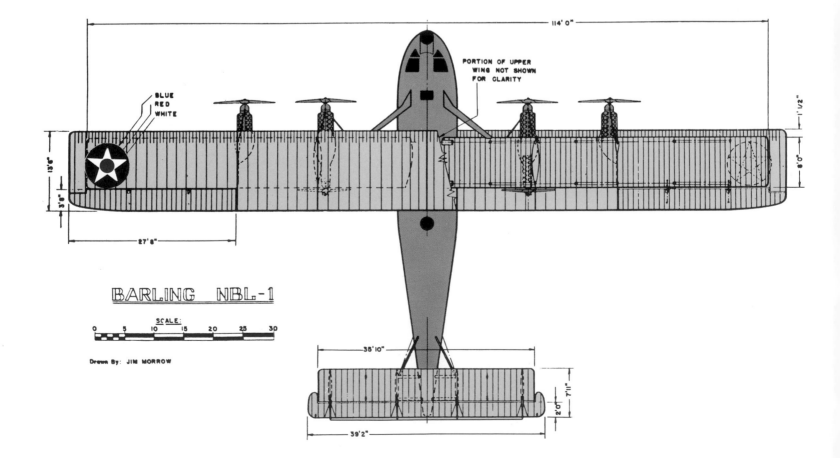

BARLING NBL-1

Drawn By: JIM MORROW

TABLE OF CONTENTS

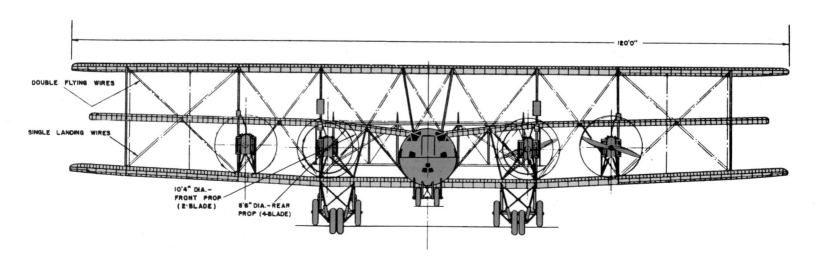

DOUBLE FLYING WIRES

SINGLE LANDING WIRES

120'0"

10'4" DIA.-
FRONT PROP
(2-BLADE)

8'6"DIA.-REAR
PROP (4-BLADE)

INTRODUCTION

The subjects of this book are not the greats, nor the near greats, of aviation history, but the black sheep that have embarrassed their builders, enraged their owners and frightened their pilots. In many cases, these are aircraft that should never have been built, and which are more starkly bizarre than the most deranged flights of fantasy. Such aircraft are made ever so much worse simply by the fact that *someone* once actually took them *seriously*.

Our inclusions have been selected on the basis of their having utterly failed at their intended role, or their having been built or conceived for an utterly ill-conceived task. We have included aircraft that were designed to be overweight and underpowered despite existing aeronautical knowledge — or even despite ordinary common sense. Some of our selections were designed — by people who should have known better — as being virtually impossible to get off the ground, while others herein were designed to be impossible to land!

We have also included such aircraft as the Super DC-3 and the F-20 Tigershark, which would have been good — perhaps great — had they not been so completely and utterly cursed with bad timing. Included too are aircraft like the XA2D Skyshark, whose engines were so bad that they made the airplanes themselves not simply mediocre, but deadly.

Finally, we concluded with Northrop's B-2 Stealth bomber, not because we felt like whipping Northrop at the end of the book, but because a major American newsmagazine picked out the B-2, on the eve of her maiden flight, to head a list of America's 'Worst Weapons.' For this reason we decided to put the B-2 on the table, when in fact, by 1989, it had yet to prove itself 'bad' in any category except price tag.

We have excluded aircraft that have overcome horrible — and

Facing page: The arrogant Icarus of Greek mythology developed the world's first worst aircraft and wound up in the Aegean Sea. *Above:* Though it has a good record, the McDonnell Douglas DC-10 suffered two disastrous crashes in 1974 and 1979, which led to many people refusing to book flights aboard such aircraft.

Below: The deHavilland Comet was the world's first jetliner, but a series of crashes beginning in 1952 undermined the public's confidence in it and cost the Comet a leading role in commercial aviation, despite the fact that its shortcomings had been corrected.

often unwarranted—reputations. Certainly this category must feature the McDonnell Douglas DC-10, which almost killed the company when it suffered two terrible and media-grabbing crashes during the 1970s. At the time, these were the worst air disasters in civil aviation history. These disasters gave the DC-10 an image of being the *Titanic* of the airways and almost put the Douglas half of McDonnell Douglas out of business. However, the crashes were attributed to sloppy maintenance rather than an inherent design defect, and the fact that they were the worst crashes in civil aviation history had to do with the fact that planes in the large, wide-body, 'jumbo' jet class were still a recent innovation, and no plane with over 200 people had ever been lost prior to the 1974 and 1979 DC-10 crashes. With so much blood on its hands, the DC-10 became an international pariah, but millions of successive non-fatal DC-10 miles restored that bird's reputation, only to have it come into question after two dreadful crashes during July 1989. In these crashes, in which over half the passengers survived, factors such as pilot error and questionable maintenance, rather than design defects, were found to be at fault.

World War II fostered a great many terrible mistakes in the aviation field. Certain specific aircraft are brought to mind, such as the RAF's dreadfully underpowered, unreliable and unpopular Avro Manchester and Bristol Blenheim 5. We have chosen to omit them, however, because, if nothing else, the Manchester was a stepping stone to the great Lancaster, while the Blenheim 5 was merely a black sheep in a distinguished line.

In the immediate postwar years there was a spurt of less-than-perfect aircraft, but we've chosen to exclude the simply mediocre and focus on the real blunders, such as the XP-87, which helped to destroy the great Curtiss legacy, and the Saunders-Roe Princess and McDonnell Goblin that epitomized untenable concepts.

Since prehistory, humans have—in their infinite species arrogance—envied few of God's other creatures. Birds are certainly the exception. The quest for flight is as old as mankind's inherent urge to emulate the birds and 'slip the surly bonds' of planet Earth.

Because man is cursed with the anatomical inconvenience brought about by his lack of wings, he has had to make do with prostheses and machines, and therein begins our tale. The history of our quest for flight was filled with a catalogue of hopeful might-have-beens and preposterous blunders and prevarications. In short, the world was full of a lot of *worst* aircraft long before there were any *other* kind of aircraft!

The archetypical first worst attempt at flight—the 'granddaddy of them all'— was Icarus, the lad of Grecian myth, who constructed a set of wings using feathers and wax. The scenario was an escape from the island of Crete to the Greek mainland, and as the story goes, poor Icarus flew too close to the sun, whereupon the wax melted and the whole scheme came apart (pun intended).

Gliding—the challenge of real-life Icari—was attempted without success during the Middle Ages and the Renaissance, while at the same time, people like Leonardo da Vinci were working on the ultimate goal: *controlled, powered* flight in a *heavier-than-air* vehicle—literally, an airplane.

Lighter-than-air flight—ballooning—came first, however. Balloons themselves predate the fourteenth century, but the first

Right: The Douglas X-3 Stiletto, first flown in 1952, looked very fast, but wasn't. Intended to explore the supersonic flight environment, it never got past Mach .98 because of its sluggish powerplant.

known successful balloon ride by human beings involves the brothers Joseph Michel and Jacques Etienne Montgolfier at Annonay, France in 1783. In Germany, Otto Lilienthal became the first man to fly a successful glider in 1891, but still the problem of controlled, powered flight in a heavier-than-air vehicle remained elusive.

By the time of Lilienthal's flight, basic aerodynamic principals that had begun with Leonardo, had been identified, resolved and refined. Thus the principal problem on the road to practical airplanes, was the problem of a practical powerplant. Indeed, it was later discovered that Leonardo's fifteenth century airplane would have worked if he'd had access to a 5 hp lawn mower motor!

In the early nineteenth century, In the wake of the Montgolfier's success in the balloon field, Sir George Cayley in England began tinkering with a steam-powered airplane. On its face, the idea of a delicate kite-like machine attempting to loft a huge cast iron steam engine and a boiler full of water seems like a good candidate for our pantheon of 'worst' aircraft. However, in 1848, Cayley's protégés, Bill Henson and John Stringfellow, actually succeeded in achieving powered flight with a small-scale model. Attempts to repeat the experiment with a man-carrying variant, however, didn't meet with the same success.

Thus it is that we have chosen to begin our survey in 1903, the year that powered, heavier-than-air flight became a proven reality. Our list is by no means encyclopedic—it really cannot be—because there is by definition a great deal of subjectivity in any survey that pretends to enumerate the worst or best of anything. This list is not intended to be exhaustive, simply because it is really impossible to quantify the characteristics that have driven aircraft into these halls of shame. Some aircraft—such as the Tarrant Tabor, Capronisimo or Christmas Bullet—would be on almost anyone's 'worst' list (just as the

DC-3 or the Spitfire would make almost any survey of the best), while others included here may be aircraft that many people never thought of as 'bad.' On the other hand, there are some which I may seem to have forgotten. Some of these are ones that I purposely excluded, while others may be ones that I simply didn't think worthy of mention. James Gilbert included man-powered aircraft among his 'worst' but I disagree. They may be silly and impractical on one hand, but they are noble efforts by pioneering eccentrics, not airplanes that the world would have been better off without.

Furthermore, the list is also restricted to heavier-than-air, fixed-wing aircraft that were actually built and flight-tested. It would be interesting to include such lighter-than-air monstrosities as the British R-101 airship or the German *Hindenberg*; or such as the Sikorsky H-53 series of helicopters that have proven themselves to be too complex to accomplish many of their designated missions, and in some cases too complex to even remain in the air. It would also be tempting to pull some turkeys from the drawing boards, so as to bring in such wonders as the Skoda Kauba, a jet fighter being developed in Czechoslovakia during the waning years of the Third Reich that was to be fueled by none other than coal slurry!

On the subject of inclusions or exclusions, I fully expect—and indeed welcome—reader mail. It is not my intention to unduly ridicule any planemakers—except maybe in the case of Count Caproni or Dr Christmas, but to poke lighthearted fun at some human eccentricities, and to shake an occasional finger at institutions such as General Motors for hoodwinking the US Government with the XP-75. The purpose then, really, is to make a tour of monuments to both foolishness and bad timing, and to have a little fun in so doing.

Bill Yenne
August 1989

Above: The only one of its species ever built, this forlorn bird was McDonnell's only non-government program prior to the merger with Douglas. First flown in 1959, the Model 220 was supposed to compete with Lockheed's Jetstar and North American's Sabreliner, but despite the herculean sales efforts, not one was sold. *Below:* Seen in Cleveland in 1938, a pilot ponders the possibility of taking off in his ungainly Abrams Explorer.

Prior to World War II, military transport aircraft were few, and light on payload. They were usually adaptations of civilian airliners such as the American DC-3 or the German Ju-52. During the war, however, they grew ridiculously as though they could expand infinitely.

Below: The Lockheed Model 89 Constitution was originally designed for Pan American World Airways to fulfill a wartime US Navy contract to haul men and materiel to the Pacific Theater. When it finally made its first flight in 1946, it was underpowered by nearly half because it had to rely on Pratt & Whitney Twin Wasp piston engines instead of the turboprops that were originally specified, but never delivered. The Navy bought the XR6V-1, but cancelled the production series. The huge, albeit underpowered, XR6V-1s could carry nearly 200 troops up to 4500 miles, but they served most memorably as public relations instruments.

Far right: The Convair Model 37 was developed in parallel to the Constitution and delivered to the US Air Force as XC-99. Like the Constitution, it was a product of wartime requirements for huge airlift capacity that seemed to dissipate soon after the war ended. Based on Convair's B-36 bomber (the largest bomber ever built), the one and only XC-99 prototype made its first flight in 1947. With a wingspan of 230 feet and a payload capability of 50 tons or 400 troops, it would be the largest transport in the world until the debut of the Lockheed C-5A Galaxy in 1968.

Right: The Fairchild XC-120 was a development of the C-87 Packet and C-119 Flying Boxcar. Conceived as a C-119 with a detachable module, only one XC-120 was built (using C-119 parts).

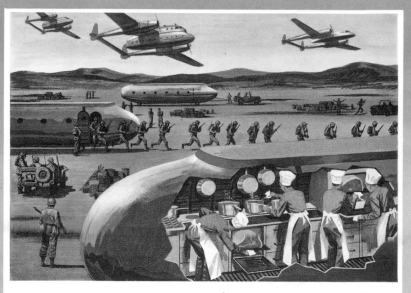

AMONG THE WORST

WORST

The Langley Aerodrome

B y the dawn of the twentieth century, aeronautical engineers—or we should say those who would soon call themselves aeronautical engineers—knew that powered, heavier-than-air flight was not only theoretically possible, it was going to become a reality *soon*.

It was against this backdrop that the Smithsonian Institution undertook a project which was very much the Project Apollo. Powered flight was possible, and the best resources of the federal government would be put on the case, and they'd *prove* it!

The best resources were, in this case, placed at the disposal of Professor Samuel Pierpont Langley, astronomer, scientist and secretary of the Smithsonian. His résumé was impeccable, and beyond this, he had himself built a 25 pound steam-powered model airplane, which he had successfully tested in 1886 in the presence of none other than the great inventor Alexander Graham Bell. If anyone was going to create the world's first practical manned airplane, it would be Samuel Pierpont Langley.

Thanks in part to Bell, President William McKinley became so enthralled with Langley, and with this historic national effort, that he pulled $50,000 out of the War Department budget to help pay for it.

The key to the powerplant problem was to get around the cumbersome weight of steam engines, so the advent of reliable,

Above: Samuel Pierpont Langley (far left) confers with Charles Manley prior to the first attempt to launch the *Aerodrome* in 1903. *Below:* The *Aerodrome* was intended to be launched from a houseboat on the Potomac River, but it failed. *Right:* Eleven years later, Glen Curtiss redesigned the *Aerodrome* but still could keep it up for only five seconds.

internal combustion gasoline engines removed the last stumbling block on the road to powered flight. Langley went to Charles Manley at Cornell University to design his engine. They started with a quarter-scale model of both the engine and the airplane, which they successfully flew in 1901.

A great deal of care went into the full-sized craft, which was completed in July 1903. The *Aerodrome*, as Langley called it, was powered by a five-cylinder, water-cooled Balzer engine delivering 52.4 hp and weighing 207.8 pounds. The first test flight was scheduled for 7 October 1903. Charles Manley would be at the controls of the *Aerodrome*, which would be launched from a catapult constructed atop a houseboat that was to be anchored on the Potomac River downstream from Washington, DC.

The *Aerodrome* roared off the catapult and straight into the Potomac. Manley survived unhurt, but Langley's 'infallible' *Aerodrome* had achieved not a moment of powered flight. The battered craft was pulled from the water and completely rebuilt for a second attempt two months later on 8 December. This time, the *Aerodrome*'s rear wing failed during the catapult launch, and again she went into the river. Manley was almost killed, and Samuel Pierpont Langley decided to abandon the *Aerodrome* project.

Ironically, it was just *nine days* later, on 17 December 1903, at Kill Devil Hill near Kitty Hawk, North Carolina, that Wilbur and Orville Wright achieved mankind's first, second, third *and* fourth powered flights in a heavier-than-air machine. A pair of bicycle mechanics from Dayton, Ohio, the Wrights had built their Flyer for a fraction of what had been spent on the abortive *Aerodrome*. They were also, needless to say, very much outside the mainstream of the American scientific establishment.

The Wrights were granted the patent for the invention of the airplane, and proceeded to build other successful aircraft for such customers as the US Army. In the meantime, Alexander Graham Bell put together a consortium, called the Aerial Experiment Association (AEA), with the objective of competing with the Wrights, and ultimately to build *better* airplanes. The AEA

hired the flamboyant motorcycle builder Glen Hammond Curtiss as their designer, and went to work.

Ultimately, Glen Curtiss was to become one of the most important names in American aviation, but his first attempts in 1908 for the AEA were failures. When Curtiss eventually *did* achieve powered flight in one of his creations, the Wrights sued him for patent infringement. In 1914, during the ensuing court battle, Curtiss came up with a brilliant idea: if he could prove that the Langley *Aerodrome* had in fact been a viable design, then the Wrights wouldn't deserve their patent!

Curtiss then went to the Smithsonian to see about resurrecting the *Aerodrome*. Having been embarrassed by the Wrights, the Smithsonian fathers were only too happy to cooperate with Curtiss. Dr Charles Walcott, who succeeded Langley as secretary of the institution after the latter's death in 1906, arranged for the remains of the *Aerodrome* and necessary blueprints to be sent to Curtiss at his Hammondsport, New York, headquarters.

Based on his own practical experience, Curtiss quickly realized that the *Aerodrome* really *wasn't* capable of flight. However, he could also see *why* it wasn't, and he set about redesigning it. The redesigned *Aerodrome* stayed aloft for only five seconds, and it was not until Curtiss retrofitted it with a 1914-vintage V-8 engine, that he was able to achieve a minute of powered flight.

Having done this, Curtiss and Walcott returned the *Aerodrome* to its original unflyable 1903 configuration and it was placed on display at the Smithsonian Institution as 'the first man-carrying aeroplane in the history of the world capable of sustained free flight.' In fact, it was just an elaborate fraud perpetrated on both the Wrights *and* Langley. It was a deception that made the *Aerodrome* the first, and perhaps one of the worst, of the world's worst aircraft.

The Wrights had created a monument to American ingenuity, but in so doing they had profoundly embarrassed the Washington elite. It would not be until 1948 that the Wright Flyer became part of the collection and display at the Smithsonian Institution—together with an apology.

The Aerial Experiment Association *Cygnet II*

Despite the forthcoming *Aerodrome* hoax, Glen Curtiss was on his way to becoming the world's second great aircraft designer. In 1908, his *June Bug*, which was built under the auspices of Alexander Graham Bell's Aerial Experiment Association, won the *Scientific American* Trophy as the first airplane to cover a straight-line distance of one kilometer

Meanwhile, Dr Bell himself, now 61, was anxious for one final grand invention to anchor the golden years of his lifetime of achievement. This was to be AEA's fifth aircraft, a bizarre monstrosity that Dr Bell dubbed *Cygnet II*, taking as its name-

sake the AEA's 1907 glider, the *Cygnet*. To quote Louis S Casey, a recent curator of aircraft at the Smithsonian's National Air & Space Museum, the *Cygnet II* was 'to be rather charitable in description... a very ungainly aircraft.'

Casey went on to add that 'the mass of small, rectangular surfaces that composed the tetrahedral design makes one wonder why anyone should have hoped to get it airborne. To put it in very common terms... *Cygnet II* had a built-in headwind. Even the best engine of that time could not possibly have coaxed the machine into the air.'

Clearly the result of many hours of painfully exacting hand work, the *Cygnet II* had a 26-foot wingspan and weighed 950 pounds as configured for its first flight test, which was to take place on a frozen lake on 22 February 1909. It was a bright, sunshiny day and the ice pack was hard and smooth. Alexander Graham Bell was cheerful and optimistic, but nothing could save the aging genius from his flawed design.

The first attempt, and the second two days later, were disappointing failures. In deference to Dr Bell, his younger AEA colleagues built another, more conventional tetrahedral-winged aircraft in 1912, called it *Cygnet III*, and managed to get it off the ground—barely. However, the great inventor died in 1922, having seen a great deal of aviation history come to pass, but without ever having hung his shingle on a viable airplane. The project that was to have been his crowning glory turned out to be an anticlimactic demonstration of his lack of aeronautical expertise. The *Cygnet II* was, to use a metaphor, Alexander Graham Bell's swan song.

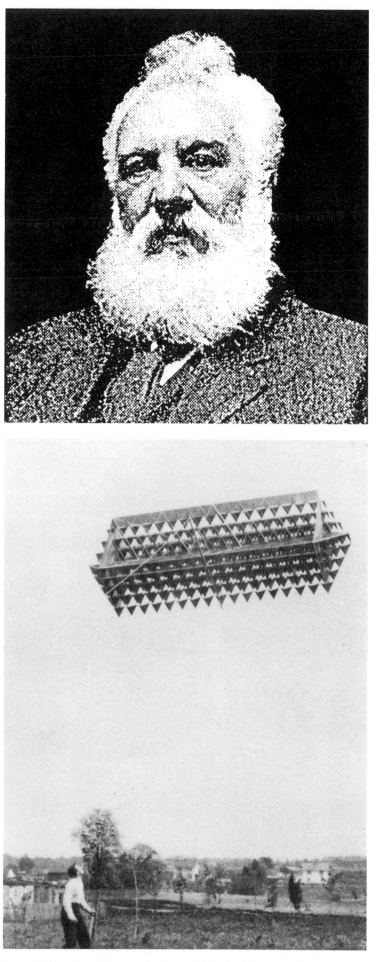

The Aerial Experiment Association Cygnet II *(left),* which was built at Badderk, Nova Scotia by the legendary inventor Alexander Graham Bell *(top)* and based on his tetrahedral kite *(above)*, was flown successfully on 15 and 18 May 1907. In the photo *at left* JAD McCurdy poses nervously at the controls prior to the 22 February 1909 flight test. The Cygnet II contained 3960 tetrahedral cells.

The Phillips Multiplanes

One clearly obvious, albeit glib, statement that we can say about aircraft designers in the years before 1910 is that they *didn't know what airplanes were supposed to look like*!

Today we have eight decades of hindsight to refer to. We *know* what airplanes are supposed to look like. In the first decade of flight, however, the whole field was so new that designers went to work without preconceived notions of the final form. Should they build airplanes that looked like birds? Like Wright Flyers? Like something completely different?

Since 1910—with notable exceptions from Sopwith and Fokker—most airplanes have been either biplanes or monoplanes, with the latter predominating after 1930. Before 1910, though, nobody knew that this was a rule. The Wright Flyer had been a biplane, but that didn't necessarily mean that *all* airplanes had to be biplanes. After all, if two pairs of wings were good, wouldn't three or four sets of wings be better? If so, what about 12 or even *a hundred* sets of wings?

Enter the multiplane designers.

The idea for the serious multiplane actually dates back to Horatio Phillips' strange machine that this eccentric English inventor attempted to flight test at Harrow in May of 1893. Powered by a steam engine (not his first mistake), this first Phillips Multiplane was unmanned and had 50 narrow wings arranged like the slats of a venetian blind. Like Cayley's earlier steam-powered unmanned aircraft, the Phillips creation managed to get off the ground, although just barely.

In 1904, just a year after the Wrights' successful first flight, Phillips built a 20-wing multiplane powered by a 22 hp, four-cylinder, inline engine of his own design. The venetian-blind-like wing surfaces spanned 17 feet 9 inches, and stood 10 feet high. The first flight test at Streatham demonstrated that the noble experiment was uncontrollable and unflyable. Undaunted, Phillips tried again in 1907 with a 200-wing multiplane, but managed a flight of only 490 feet.

Horatio Phillips may well have been the premier example of the multiplane exponent, but he was not the last. In 1908, a year after his last attempt, both Roshon in the United States and D'Equevilly in France unveiled their own variations on this preposterous theme. The Roshon machine was an exercise in absurdity. It consisted of two sets of 13 wings spaced about two feet apart and mounted on what appeared to be an old fashioned metal bed frame. Its initial flight test consisted of violent, uncontrollable hopping, followed by the complete collapse of the entire airframe like a house of cards. It was the swan song of the multiplane era.

Left: Horatio Phillips designed his multiplanes in the years before 1910 when people didn't yet know what airplanes were supposed to look like. Indeed, they were so much more genteel, with the ambiance of a Victorian drawing room with their ceiling fans and venetian blinds. Imagine the airliners of today if this design philosophy had prevailed.

Perhaps one of the most serious drawbacks to Phillips' notion of air travel was his elliptical racetrack runway. Built of carefully fitted wooden planks, it presumed that an airplane would *spiral* upward before the pilot got dizzy and lost control. Perhaps his idea was to conserve space so that people could have runways in their gardens.

The Royal Aircraft Factory BE.9 'Pulpit'

It was probably predictable that when government agencies like Britain's Royal Aircraft Factory or America's Army Engineering Division got into the business of designing airplanes, the result would be horrific. To be perfectly fair to the Royal Aircraft Factory, however, they *did* design the FE.2 that shot down Max Immelman's Fokker in 1916. Nevertheless, while the FE.2 was coping with the German Albatros fighters over the Western Front, the BE.9 was itself an *albatross* around the neck of the RAF, that would ultimately drag it into oblivion.

The BE.9 was a 1915 fighter adaptation of the BE.2 bomber that positioned a gunner in a 'pulpit' in the plane's nose ahead of the propeller. While gunner positions in the noses of airplanes are not an uncommon feature, the fact that there was no shielding between gunner and prop made this hazardous duty indeed.

The gunner would have to hang onto his Lewis gun, literally for dear life, to keep from being sucked into the whirling blades. At the same time, the location of the engine made it impossible for the gunner to communicate with the pilot on the other side.

The BE.9 had a length of 30 feet, a wing span of about 32 feet, and the deadly propeller was spun by a 90 hp RAF engine. Originally earmarked for No16 Squadron, the BE.9 was never placed into production, a decision that was applauded by Royal Flying Corps gunners that were saved from being killed or maimed by this ridiculous design.

In his *British Aeroplanes 1914-1918*, JM Bruce quotes Grinnell-Milne as saying that 'even in 1915 when almost every new machine was looked at with delighted wonder, it was recognized that in the BE.9 unsuitability of design had reached its acme.'

Below: The Royal Aircraft Factory 'Pulpit' isolated the gunner ahead of the engine so that he had to communicate with the pilot through the spinning prop. The BE.9 was the original 'white knuckle' airplane, for it was also necessary for the gunner to hang onto his gun tightly to avoid being sucked into the blades that whirled noisily a few inches behind his head.

The Royal Aircraft Factory BE.12 and The Royal Aircraft Factory RE.8

The acme of bad design at the Royal Aircraft Factory (RAF) may well have been reached in 1916 with the dreadful BE.9, but the BE.12 and RE.8 proved that the faultiness of the BE.9 was not the only time during the Great War that this venerable institution dropped the ball.

The BE.12 was a single-seat fighter that eventually was used as a bomber. It had a wingspan of 37 feet and a length of 27 feet 3 inches. Based on the BE.2c, it was powered—or we should say underpowered—by a 150 hp RAF engine. The problem was that the BE.12 took three quarters of an hour to struggle up to 10,000 feet, hardly ideal for a fighter. Furthermore, once it reached altitude, it couldn't hold the height without a struggle. The RAF had delivered 468 of these miserable machines before the commander of the Royal Flying Corps (RFC) finally said 'enough' and refused to accept any more.

The RE.8 was a two-place reconnaissance machine with a wingspan of 42 feet 7 inches and a length of 27 feet 10.5 inches. It was 'underpowered' by the same unreliable 150 hp engine used in the BE.12 and was equally hard to keep up. Beyond this, the RE.8 was a veritable catalogue of bad design features. It was hard to maneuver in combat, yet its small tail made it prone to uncontrollable spins. The engine was installed in such a way that pilots had a hard time seeing over it while landing and the fuel tank was located so close to the engine that it would often catch fire.

If a pilot managed to avoid being shot down, spinning out of control or catching fire, the RAF added one more insult by making the RE.8 hard to land!

Below: You can almost sense the panic in the eyes of this poor Royal Flying Corps pilot who will soon take off in his rickety RE.8. One wonders about the admonishment of a minimum weight requirement in the gunner's compartment being the largest lettering on the fuselage apart from the tail number. One also wonders where the 150-pound gunner was when this photo was taken.

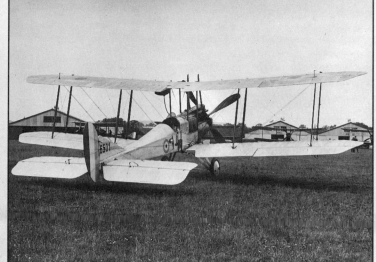

Left: Variations of the BE.12 at a Royal Flying Corps base circa 1918. The stacks, whether channeled into a Y or left independent, were designed to thrust soot and carbon monoxide up and away from the pilot.

Below: An RE.8 somewhere in France in 1917. Like those of the BE.12, the engine stacks resembled a farm tractor's. There is little wonder the pilots pictured in photographs of RE.8s always look so apprehensive.

The Albatros D-5

Albatros Flugzeug Werke GmbH came into the forefront of German aviation early in World War I. If one recalls that Anthony Herman Fokker, the greatest designer of Axis airplanes during the era, was Dutch, then Albatros must be remembered as the top *German* planemaker of World War I. Indeed, men like Ernst Heinkel were on the staff at Albatros. It is precisely for this reason that the D-5 is an unforgivable blunder.

Introduced in 1917 as a successor to the highly-regarded Albatros D-3, the Albatros D-5 was 24 feet long, with a wing span of 29 feet 7 inches and a gross weight of 2013 pounds. It was a single-seat fighter armed with a pair of Spandau 7.92 mm guns. It was constructed in large numbers, over 500 of which reached the front in November 1917 alone. It was here that the dreadful drawbacks began to manifest themselves. The lower wing was weak and prone to flutter and distortion, which led to a great many fatal crashes. Attempts were made in the field to brace the wing, but it was not until someone thought to attach a metal sleeve over the spar at mid-wing that the flaw was rectified. Even then, the spar was prone to failure in steep dives.

The Fokker D-5

Anthony Herman Gerald Fokker was, without a doubt, the greatest international aircraft designer of the first quarter century of heavier-than-air flight. Born in Java in the Netherlands East Indies in 1890, Tony Fokker grew up in the Netherlands, and moved to Germany to design and build airplanes when he was barely 21. The first World War found him still in Germany and, since Holland remained neutral, he saw no conflict of interest in staying on. Despite his having built the best airplanes in the Kaiser's air force, the Germans lost the war and 'the Flying Dutchman' returned home. Eventually he also built aircraft in the United States, establishing a firm international reputation.

Fokker's German designs included his wonderful D-7, and the great Dr-1 triplane that was favored by Baron Manfred von Richthofen. Also included was the dreadful D-5. Slightly smaller than the D-7, the D-5 preceded it by about a year and a half. Introduced in 1916, it was 22.5 feet long with a wingspan of 28 feet 3 inches and a gross weight of 1245 pounds.

It was difficult to fly, with horn-balanced ailerons on a swept upper wing and inadequate tail surfaces. Designed as a fighter, it was very unpopular with pilots and was relegated to service training unsuspecting would-be pilots. If they could survive the D-5, they could survive combat. While not exactly a deathtrap like the Albatros and Royal Aircraft Factory machines discussed above, the Fokker D-5 was clearly not up to the standards that 'the Flying Dutchman' would soon set.

Left: A jolly Tony Fokker in the cockpit of his D-5 fighter, a clumsy waypoint en route to the great D-7. *Top right:* A Fokker D-5 with a 100 hp Oberosel powerplant. *Top left:* The lower wing of the Albatros D-5 would often crumple under stress like paper in the wind, bringing the whole aircraft and her pilot down in a spinning mass of tortured wreckage. Over 500 were built before this dreadful characteristic was made manifest.

The Tarrant Tabor

By the last year of World War I, military aircraft technology had evolved to the point where the Allies could realistically begin to think about developing bombers to conduct raids on Berlin. In fact, had the war continued into 1919, such an air offensive would have become a reality. The centerpiece of this effort would have been the big Vickers Vimy and Handley-Page V1500 bombers that were being developed specifically for that purpose by Britain's most experienced builders of large aircraft. These airplanes were completed before the war ended, but they never saw action against any truly strategic targets deep inside Germany.

In the meantime, however, another player had entered the field. WG Tarrant was a building contractor from Surrey whose only experience in the aviation field had been when his firm was pressed into service early in the war as a subcontractor to build wooden components for the major airplane manufacturers. He stood by quietly as the Handley-Page O100s and O400s flew over German lines to strike the Ruhr and the Saar in 1916. However, when His Majesty's government started talking about warplanes with the range to reach Berlin, it stirred Tarrant's patriotism. More than likely, it also stirred an interest in the lucrative postwar applications for an aircraft with this kind of range.

Aware that the first step in realizing his dream was to build the airplane of his dream, Tarrant sought, and won, a contract from the Royal Aircraft Establishment to build a prototype for what would be the world's largest bomber. They too realized that a long range transport would be just as important to the British Empire in the long term as bombing Berlin was in the short term.

This was probably just as well, because Tarrant did not complete his monster until several months after the Armistice. When she did emerge, though, she was a sight to behold. Given the name Tabor, she was a six-engined triplane whose top airfoil would rise higher that the roof of a four-story building. She weighed eight tons completely empty and had a wingspan of 131 feet, making her larger than any of the great heavy bombers of the *Second* World War except the B-29 Superfortress. When she was unveiled, Tarrant claimed that his Tabor could fly from England to India with but one fuelling stop.

The first flight was scheduled for 26 May 1919. Tarrant was nervous and overreactive. So much so that when it was suggested that the Tabor might be a bit tail heavy, he ordered that a half ton of lead be shovelled into her nose. This last minute modification didn't seem to bother the crew, however, who were headed by Captain FG Dunn of the Royal Flying Corps, whose résumé included a respectable number of hours in the cockpit of a Handley-Page V1500.

The take-off roll went smoothly, and Dunn throttled up the six Napier Lions. The tail lifted off the ground and it seemed as though Tarrant's worst fear had been allayed. Suddenly, however, the top two engines, located precariously high above the Tabor's center of gravity, began to pull the big plane into what amounted to a 100 mph somersault. The tail shot up and the huge aircraft nosed into the soft ground, as struts, wires and wing fragments cartwheeled past the disintegrating fuselage and scattered across the field.

It was all over in one horrible instant: the Tabor; the lives of pilot, co-pilot and flight engineer; and the grand dream of the inexperienced amateur superplane entrepreneur from Surrey.

WG Tarrant left the aviation field forever, but for one of his designers on the project—Walter H Barling—there would be another chance at stardom.

Below and opposite: WG Tarrant's huge machine was awesome to behold.

The Barling-Witteman-Lewis XNBL-1 'Barling Bomber'

Soon after the Tarrant Tabor fiasco, Walter H Barling relocated to the United States, where his ideas for further superbombers caught the ear of US Army Air Service General William L 'Billy' Mitchell. The commander of all American front line airpower during World War I, Billy Mitchell was one of history's most vocal advocates of *strategic* airpower, the doctrine of flying *over* the lines to strike the heart of the enemy's industrial war-making capability. To do this, an air force must have *big* bombers. Walter Barling talked big bombers, and Billy Mitchell liked what he heard.

During 1920, Barling designed a huge triplane, the largest bomber to fly in the United States until the eve of World War II. With a wingspan of 120 feet and a length of 65 feet, it was slightly smaller than the Tarrant Tabor, but still larger than the Flying Fortresses and Liberators of two decades hence. Barling gave his enormous creation six 400 hp Liberty 12s—two pushing and four pulling—and thoughtfully placed them all between the bottom two wings to avoid the problem that had killed the Tabor and her crew.

Built in New Jersey by Witteman-Lewis, it was given the Army designation XNBL-1 for Night Bomber, Long-range, Experimental, First. Plans had called for two prototypes, but budget cuts reduced the order to just one. Though the press came to call the XNBL-1 'Mitchell's Folly,' Mitchell and Barling were sure that their belief in the project would carry the day, and that a production series would follow.

Below and opposite: Struggling under the colossal weight of its 16-ton airframe, Walter Barling's XNBL-1 lumbers across the skies above Wright Field in Ohio at 2000 feet. Twenty long and arduous minutes into its maiden flight, the mammoth triplane reached 7000 feet, but after that the poor beast could climb no higher.

When the big aircraft was finally completed in October 1922 and transported to Wright Field in Ohio, it was the largest single object ever transported by an American railroad. It was so large that it had to be stored over the winter and reassembled during the summer of 1923.

After nearly a week of taxi tests, the Barling Bomber was flown for the first time on 22 August 1923. It lifted off in 360 fcct and struggled up to 7000 feet in 20 minutes. She was hugely underpowered, the engines overheated and the landing gear could barely support the weight, but she flew. By point of comparison, the XNBL-1 had a gross weight of 32,203 pounds supported by a total aggregate engine horsepower of 2400, whereas a World War II B-17G had a gross weight of 55,000 pounds carried by 4800 hp.

The XNBL-1's voluminous cross-laminated spruce fuselage carried a crew of six and provision for 2.5 tons of bombs. The overall project carried a price tag of $350,000, a point that did not bode well for a production contract.

The biggest problem with the XNBL-1, however, was its lack of range. In order to be effective, strategic bombers need to fly long distances, to penetrate deep within enemy territory. With its pitiful 170-mile range, the XNBL-1 hardly filled the bill. On a hypothetical mission from Washington to New York, a Barling Bomber would have had to stop for fuel five times. In a replay of the Civil War, it would have been useful, however, for Richmond, Virginia was comfortably within the range of a Washington-based XNBL-1. To hit New York, however, an enemy airbase would have to be located north of Trenton, New Jersey.

It was found that the Barling Bomber's range could be increased to 335 miles—but only if it didn't carry any bombs. What fear could that have put into the hearts of the enemy—to know that the fearsome behemoths clouding the sky had been stripped of ordnance in order to carry enough fuel? It was sort of like 'Zen and the art of strategic airpower.' When taken in the face of the $350,000 invested in the project, the War Department was hardly amused.

The XNBL-1 flight test program ended in 1925 without the big bomber ever having been liked by those who flew her. The prototype was unceremoniously burned by Wright Field commander General Hap Arnold in 1928. Walter Barling himself vanished from the scene. Within a year of the end of the test program, Billy Mitchell had been court-martialled for insubordination on another matter and was drummed out of the service. Many of those who believed in his doctrine of strategic air power —including Hap Arnold—remained, however, and it was these men who built the US Army Air Forces that won World War II. The Barling Bomber had proved itself as nothing more than a peculiar footnote on this road to war-winning strategic airpower.

Below: Walter Barling presided proudly over a test of the four Liberty 12A engines of his sprawling XNBL-1. More ballast than Barling himself would be required to get the nose down for take-off.

General Billy Mitchell was probably the only influential advocate of the project, but this was only because he was desperate to develop a heavy bomber. The XNBL-1 bomber was heavy all right, but it couldn't fly from Dayton to Pittsburgh unless it was stripped of its payload.

The US Army Engineering Division GAX

The acronym stood for 'Ground Attack, Experimental,' but the phonetic pronunciation told the story better. The GAX was born in the byzantine world of US Army bureaucracy that mirrored the world of the Royal Aircraft Factory when they had thought up the merciless BE.9 'Pulpit' during the dark days of World War I. The similarity was that a government bureaucracy was trying to do the thinking best left to entrepreneurial innovators within the private sector; the differences were that the year was 1920, not 1916, the war was over and they damn well should have known better.

In any event, it was on the very eve of the Armistice of the 'war to end all wars,' that the Engineering Division had been charged with the task of designing a heavily armed and armored ground attack aircraft to support ground forces in the field. Simple enough, it is still an important task of military airpower. However, the problem with the ill-starred GAX lay not in conception, but in its execution. Typical of the old axiom of a machine designed by committee, the GAX emerged from the Engineering Division drawing boards at Dayton, Ohio as a well armored, yet vastly underpowered, monstrosity. Over a ton of its 7532-pound weight was devoted to quarter-inch steel armor plate designed to protect the crew of three, and the GAX's two

400 hp Liberty 12 engines. The drawbacks, primarily, were twofold: the two Liberty engines, and the fact that there were only two. The two Liberty 12s were vastly inadequate for an aircraft so heavy, despite the good intentions of all that armor.

One of only a few postwar triplanes, the GAX had a wing span of 65.5 feet, and was 33 feet 7 inches long. Armed with a 37 mm Baldwin cannon and no fewer than *eight* .30 caliber Lewis machine guns, the GAX would have been a formidable weapon were it not for the fact that the Liberty 12s could get the monster up to only 85 mph, and that all of those guns had to be presided over by only *two* gunners.

The GAX probably looked good on paper—tremendous fire-power, small crew, only two engines—but anyone with experience in the just-completed World War should have known better. The first tests down at Kelly Field in Texas after the May 1920 rollout proved the pitiful GAX to be unmaneuverable on top of

the other drawbacks. It took an incredible amount of runway for the poor Liberty 12s to get the four tons of triplane off the ground, and even then the pilots complained of poor visibility because of the position of the horrible briar patch of wings and struts.

Boeing was called in on 7 June 1920 to build 20 production aircraft under the designation GA-1 (Ground Attack, First), but this contract was soon halved. All 10 were actually completed, but by 1922, the project had evolved into the GA-2, a successor which addressed at least some of the dreadful shortcomings inherent in the GAX/GA-1.

Below: Boeing's Charlie Thompson stands sheepishly before the GAX at Camp Lewis, Washington, circa 1920, when the Seattle planemaker was called upon to build ton of those overweight monsters. With its heavy plate steel gunners' tubs and only two light engines, the GAX was an example of Government bureaucracy gone mad.

Below: The Boeing GA-2 in Seattle on 19 December 1921, shortly after it was
built. It was a fitting Christmas present for the Army Engineering Division who
had compelled the Seattle planemaker to make it.

With the 37mm cannons and .50 caliber machine guns jutting from its over-
crowded gun tub, the GA-2 was a formidable weapons system. However, it was
very much like Vietnam-era helicopters in that its armor could shield the crew but
not the delicate structures that kept the craft airborne.

The Boeing GA-2

After the US Army grudgingly accepted the folly of their own Engineering Division's GAX, which had become the Boeing GA-1 (Boeing Model 10) that was inflicted upon Boeing, the GA-2 (also built as Boeing Model 10) became the compromise which was seen as the salvation for a project that should, quite simply, have been terminated. Nevertheless, the Army and Boeing plowed forward with the GA-2 in late 1921. The GA-1 was clearly a mistake on its own (lack of) merits, but the GA-2 was twice the mistake, because everyone involved should have known better *because* of the GAX/GA-1 debacle.

The Boeing GA-2 would have been an acceptable piece of mediocrity had it not been for its predecessors. It was a 37-foot-long biplane with a wing span of 54 feet and an empty weight of 6784 pounds. Powered by a single 700 hp Engineering Division W-1A-18 water-cooled engine, it repeated one of its father's most unforgivable flaws—lack of power!

Like the GAX/GA-1, the GA-2 had a crew of three that was horribly over-worked in an attempt to operate a 37 mm cannon, five .50 caliber and two .30 caliber machine guns. Once again it was an aircraft that was vastly over-armored for the horsepower of its engines. Whereas the GAX/GA-1 had carried 2000 pounds of armor with a total of 800 hp, the GA-2 carried 1600 pounds of armor with 700 hp.

Only two GA-2s were built, but they stand today as among the worst aircraft ever to slip through the fingers of a manufacturer that would eventually distinguish itself with some of the best aerial bombardment weapons in the history of warfare. Live and learn.

The Loening PW-2

During the First World War, the US Army relied entirely on foreign-built machines as first-line combat aircraft. It had been that there simply hadn't been time for the domestic aircraft industry to gear up to meet the need. It was much more expedient to buy French SPADs and British Sopwiths. Not only were they battle-tested in the first three years of the war, but they were *built* in Europe, so there was no need to transport them to the theater of conflict.

After the war, despite drastic budget cuts, the Army undertook to nurture a home-grown warplane industry that had begun to flourish before the Armistice.

Like many others, Grover Loening got his start during World War I, building subassemblies for other peoples' airplanes. In 1921, four years after he'd opened his shop, Loening was still in business—with designs of his own. His first, the M-8 monoplane fighter, had actually been built in 1918, but the end of the war was also the end of the US Army's interest in seeing this plane go into service.

In 1921, however, the Army was ready to commission a new series of fighters, and Loening received an order for such an aircraft, to be built under the designation PW-2 (Pursuit, Water-cooled engine, Second). Like the M-8, the PW-2 was a high-wing monoplane. Delivered in September 1921, the two original prototypes had a pair of vertical stabilizers, but they intended to be followed by 10 PW-2As with more conventional single tails. The PW-2A had wingspan of 39 feet 9 inches, an inch more than the PW-2, and a length of 26 feet, nearly two feet greater than the prototypes. Like the PW-2, the PW-2A weighed 1876 pounds (with a gross of 2800) and was powered by a 322 hp Wright H engine. Also like the prototypes, the PW-2A had the wing attached to the fuselage in such a way that it gave the pilot almost *no* forward visibility.

The lack of visibility was only a minor inconvenience for Lieutenant Harold Harris during his flight aboard one of the first PW-2As on 20 October 1922. High over the Ohio countryside, the PW-2A suddenly decided to make up for the poorly-positioned wing by shedding it entirely!

Harris, who suddenly found himself in a wingless airplane, thus became the first American to escape from a stricken aircraft by parachute. The pilot survived, but the PW-2A program did not. This unfortunate milestone became the epitaph for Grover Loening's dreams of a place in the pantheon of aviation greats.

The Curtiss PW-8

Glen Curtiss, the Wright Brothers' old nemesis from a decade before, had developed the US Army's leading wartime training plane, the JN-series Jenny, and after 1920, quickly emerged as America's premier builder of pursuit planes. It was a primacy that they were to enjoy almost until the eve of World War II, with a long succession of fighters known generically as the 'Curtiss Hawks.'

This great lineage did, however, get off to a rather inauspicious start. In 1922, Curtiss completed work on a sleek little biplane fighter ordered by the Army under the designation PW-8 (Pursuit, Water-cooled engine, Eighth). First flown in January 1923, it was officially accepted by the Army three months later. The PW-8 was 22 feet 6 inches long, with a wingspan of 32 feet and a gross weight of 2784 pounds (the second prototype, also of 1923, weighed 3151). It had a cruising speed of 160 mph and a range of 440 miles. It was this range that gave a PW-8 the central role in Lieutenant Russell Maughan's famous transcontinental flight.

Despite their durability and capability, the first PW-8s carried a horrendous design flaw. The twin radiators for the 440 hp Curtiss D-12 engine were located on *top* of the wing. This was all very well and good—unless one or both of them sprung a

leak. Somehow, the person responsible for this monstrous feature had assumed that it was impossible for these precariously-placed cauldrons to be hit by a bullet during aerial combat. Should that have happened, however, the pilot would have been inundated by a torrent of scalding water to die in a horrible, medieval ordeal.

Ultimately, Curtiss corrected this problem, moved the radiator, and went on to build 25 PW-8s.

Below: The Loening PW-2 offered pitifully poor visibility for a pursuit ship, but its real Achilles' heel was its poorly attached wing. *Right:* Lt Maughan heads west in his Curtiss PW-8. By the time Maughan made his historic flight, Curtiss had corrected the problematical placement of the radiators.

The Boeing XP-9

As the science and art of aeronautics matured in the late 1920s, Boeing was on the verge of claiming the distinction of being a world leader in both the fields of military and commercial aircraft, but there was one final stumbling block on the road to superstardom, and this was a wicked little US Army Air Corps fighter known as XP-9 for Pursuit, Experimental, Ninth.

The XP-9 was not Boeing's first US Army fighter—there had been the PW-9, P-4, P-7 and P-8—but it was Boeing's first *monoplane* fighter, an innovation in an era where biplanes were the standard. Built as Boeing Model 96 under a $60,000 contract signed in June 1928, the prototype XP-9 was 25 feet 8 inches long, with a wing span of 36 feet 7 inches, making it slightly larger than the Army's previous Boeing pursuit ships.

The same ratio held for its gross weight of just over 3600 pounds. Power was supplied by a 600 hp Curtiss V-1570, similar to that employed in the P-7 prototype.

With a top speed of roughly 200 mph, the XP-9 probably looked good on the spec sheet, but when it came time for the initial test flight in November 1930, the poor beast's major drawback emerged. The huge wing—more than six feet across—was located at the top of the fuselage immediately ahead of the cockpit, which restricted the pilot's downward

Below: Though its open cockpit afforded somewhat better visibility than Loening's PW-2, the Boeing XP-9 was a 'menace' to land. Wisely, the Army chose not to order the XP-9 into production.

visibility to practically nil. Not only did this characteristic severely hamper the XP-9's operational capability, it made landing a hazardous maneuver. The test pilot is remembered for calling the XP-9 a 'menace.'

As with the three earlier Boeing fighters, the Army chose not to order the XP-9 into production, and the prototype wound up as a contribution to land fill somewhere near Wright Field. As for Boeing, they went back to the drawing board—and back to the biplane configuration—and created their Model 101, which the Army *did* order into production. Produced under the P-12 designation, the Model 101 begat one of the best and most successful series of Army fighters in the interwar period.

The Christmas Bullet

To those who first met him, the lively and dapper Dr Christmas was a friend indeed for a time of need—the man who would make the new and reckless world of aviation a safer and better one for all mankind. In the 20/20 hindsight of history, however, William Christmas, of Warrenton, North Carolina, was perhaps the greatest charlatan to ever see his name associated with an airplane.

We say perhaps, because even today it is hard to figure whether the good doctor (they say that he really *was* a doctor of medicine) was a fraud and a scoundrel, or just a naive eccentric.

In any case, he arrived on the scene in 1918 with a fanciful tale about having built and flown airplanes as early as 1907, and about having established his Christmas Aeroplane Company in 1912. Somehow, though, there was nobody that could be found who had ever seen a Christmas Aeroplane—in the air, or on the ground. His objective in 1918 was to construct an aircraft for the purpose of kidnapping Kaiser Wilhelm II of Germany. This was despite his story of having been offered a million dollars in gold in 1914 to 'take over' Germany's aircraft development.

Incredibly, he had little trouble convincing a number of people

that he was not only an experienced aviation pioneer, but fully able to carry out the abduction of the Kaiser. This being the dark depths of World War I, there was probably at least a little wishful thinking involved.

First to fall under his spell were Alfred and Henry McCrory of the New York brokerage firm of the same name, who promptly enlisted the support of Senator James Wadsworth in obtaining aircraft engines—hard to obtain in wartime—for the project. Meanwhile, the nearly-bankrupt Continental Aircraft Company of Amityville, Long Island was enlisted to build the airframe to Dr Christmas' specifications. Eventually Senator Wadsworth convinced the Army to supply an engine, but they did so with the caveat that they allow the Army to see and test the airplane before it was flown.

The 'specifications' that Dr Christmas had in mind (he was afraid to commit them to paper) were so bizarre that even the Continental people—who were desperate for business—thought twice. Simply put, he was breaking every rule in the book. His overriding theory of aircraft design was that struts and bracing should be eliminated, and that the wings should be so flexible that they could literally flap like a bird's! To top this unorthodoxy, Dr Christmas insisted on constructing his airplane of steel and hardwood.

Now nicknamed 'Bullet' for no obvious reason, the Christmas aircraft was completed in the fall of 1918, but the war ended before it could be flown. One problem was that the doctor

Below: A good candidate for being the worst aircraft ever flown, the Christmas Bullet was more a murder weapon than an airplane. Escape by parachute was impossible because the Bullet disintegrated before it got high enough for a parachute to be useful.

couldn't find a pilot. One by one they looked it over, tried the controls and walked away shaking their heads. Finally, Dr Christmas was able to lure a pigeon from among the ranks of the unemployed Army Air Service pilots returning from the war.

Ironically, it was just after Christmastime in 1918 when Cuthbert Mills took the Christmas Bullet up for her maiden flight. He got it airborne successfully, but within moments the flimsy wings twisted and peeled from the heavy fuselage and the Bullet fell like a lead projectile, taking Mills to his death. Undaunted, Christmas hardly broke stride. Even though he had flown the Bullet without telling the Army—as he'd promised—

and had destroyed their engine, he had no qualms about going back to them in February 1919 to ask for help getting a propeller for his second Bullet.

In March 1919, Christmas put the second Bullet on display at the New York Air Show, where he had the audacity to advertise it as the 'safest, easiest controlled plane in the world.' It was the same airplane that was destined to destroy a barn and a second test pilot's life when it was flown for the first time.

In a stereotypical morality play, Christmas would have been unmasked and duly punished. In fact, he simply went on to still grander prevarications, even going so far as to go before the US

Congress to tell them that his Bullets were the fastest, safest and most efficient airplanes on Earth, and that he was being swamped by orders from Europe. In actual fact, there were no orders—and indeed no Bullets! This didn't bother Dr Christmas, who in 1923 impudently billed the US Army $100,000 for his 'revolutionary' wing design. He had to have had a gift of charm that has been exceeded by few men in history. The Army paid the bill.

Dr William Christmas died quietly in 1960 at age 94 with money in his pockets and blood on his hands. His was the kind of tale that they used to write folk songs about.

Below: They called him Dr William Whitney Christmas, though that may not have been his name, and his medical diploma probably reached him by mail order. His airplane was called the Bullet Biplane, although its plywood hull resembled a wedge of cheese. Its wings, designed to flap like those of a bird, defied controllability and simply refused to stay attached to the airplane once it became airborne.

In March 1919, three months after the first Bullet *(seen here)* killed its pilot, Christmas took a display at the New York Air Show for his Cantilever Aero Company, which he used as a platform to advertise the identical and yet unflown second Bullet as the 'safest' in the world. It was later to kill its pilot on its first flight.

The Caproni Ca-60 Transaereo 'Capronisimo'

It was a true case of an airplane company that clearly should have known better, but it wound up being the story of perhaps the worst airplane that ever took wing.

With the huge Ca-31/Ca-32 bombers that he built for the Italian air force in 1914 and 1915, Count Caproni developed a reputation for having produced the largest warplanes outside Tsarist Russia. They had wingspans greater than 72 feet, and gross weights in the four ton range, with half-ton bomb capacities. This series, which evolved into the more powerful and more capable Ca-33, accounted for production totals in excess of 400 aircraft, an impressive tally for such large aircraft in this era. The subsequent Ca-42 triplane had nearly twice the gross weight and spanned nearly 100 feet.

All of this is by way of saying that Caproni was on solid footing in the field of large airplanes. The firm built literally hundreds for service with Italy during World War I, and licenses were granted for further production in the United States, as well as Britain and France.

After the war, it was not to be unexpected that the airplane builders who had built the biggest warplanes would start to plan commercial aircraft that could carry dozens, or even hundreds, of passengers. The ultimate prize was, as it would continue to be, the North Atlantic market linking Europe's great cities with New York. Ultimately it would be a dozen years after the *next* World War before airliners with hundred-passenger capacities would routinely fly the route, but in 1920, the dream seemed much closer.

Count Caproni was one of those who dreamed the dream, but

the substance of his vision looked to the rest of the world like a nightmare, a hallucination, or even just a joke. It is remarkable that anyone would have ever actually built such a thing. The Count built his airplane, which he designated Ca-60, and named Transaereo, on Lake Maggiore, beginning with a 77-foot, flat-sided houseboat. With a deluxe interior, and plenty of window space, the Transaereo was a nice houseboat that could have happily plied the waters of Lake Maggiore for years, had not the Count harbored the passion to fly it to New York.

To accomplish his goal, Caproni needed wings. Some of his big wartime machines had been triplanes—more lifting area to lift bigger loads. However, his biggest bombers had weighed 15,000 pounds. The Transaereo would weigh 55,000 pounds! No problem, he thought as he attached not one, not two, but *three* sets of triplane wings to his houseboat. Measuring 98 feet from tip to tip, each set was essentially identical, and indeed, they looked as though they could have been simply pulled from a trio of Ca-42s. To power the Ca-60—which now weighed more than three times as much as the Ca-42—Caproni selected eight American-built 400 hp Liberty V12 engines.

With the cabin fitted out for 100 passengers, the plane that was now being called 'Capronisimo' was completed early in 1921, the largest airplane of its kind yet built. On 4 March, before a host of dignitaries, the Transaereo made her maiden—and final—flight. Somehow, the 3200 horses managed to drag the 23-ton monstrosity 60 feet out of the water before the ballast scudded into her nose, the center wing section crumpled and the 'Capronisimo' plummeted back into the lake in a hail of broken and splintering wood.

In the aftermath, there was some talk about the pilot having taken her down deliberately in order to save himself from certain death when—not if—the Ca-60 failed at a higher altitude, and to save the 100 passengers from their inevitable fate over the North Atlantic. Caproni promised to rebuild his 'Capronisimo,' but there was a fire of 'mysterious' origin, which destroyed that part of the machine which had been salvaged and pulled up on shore after the crash.

For Count Caproni this was the end. With no war to fight, and his reputation for commercial aircraft thoroughly blackened, he skulked back into oblivion.

Below: Count Caproni's Ca-60 Transaereo parked proudly on Lake Maggiore, 4300 miles east of New York City. The Count dreamed of flying his huge, converted houseboat to New York. It never made it, and Caproni's dream literally went up in smoke.

Below: You could almost hear the strains of a Verdi opera as the curtain rose and the 'Capronisimo' glided gracefully from its hanger on the banks of Lake Maggiore. The proud crew posed defiantly as the photographer recorded the event for posterity.

A virtual jungle of struts, the huge machine was then carefully pulled down the rails into the lake as the photographer grabbed his satchel and plates. A few weeks later, on 4 March 1921, the rickety monster creaked into the air only to crumble into a mass of broken matchsticks long short of the glory of Count Caproni's grand dreams.

The Kalinin K-7 and Tupolev Ant-20

The dream of huge transports capable of carrying large numbers of passengers found fertile ground in many countries, but never really bore fruit until after the Second World War. Between the wars—in addition to the dreadful 'Capronisimo'—there were a number of big transport aircraft designed in Europe and America, but only a handful were ever built, and none of the really big dreams (100+ passengers) ever actually went into service.

There was Claudius Dornier's big Do-X of 1929 which could carry 150 passengers, but it took her *10 months* to fly from Germany to New York on a demonstration flight in 1930-31. The Pan Am Clippers (built by Martin, Sikorsky and later Boeing) succeeded in conquering the airways on a global scale in the years immediately before World War II, but the biggest of them, the Boeing 314, could carry only 74 passengers.

Among those which *were* built, there were few stranger than the Kalinin K-7 and the Tupolev Ant-20. It was strange on one hand because of the fact that so ponderous and clumsy aircraft could actually fly, and on the other hand because the big craft were developed in the Soviet Union during the Stalin years. It would seem that within the context of Josef Stalin's paranoid quest for socialist egalitarianism, so grand a concept as a 120-passenger airliner would have no place. However, Stalin and his cronies, for all the lip service they paid to the 'proletariat,' were consummate showmen more interested in the glory of the Soviet State than in the everyday lives of Russian peasants. In this context, grandiose machines of unique design had a very important political role.

Konstantin Kalinin began his career as a pilot in Tsar Nicholas II's air force during World War I. He joined the Bolsheviks in 1917 and went on to serve them both as a pilot and as a repair shop boss before he started designing aircraft in 1925. His early designs were rather standard transport types, consisting mainly of high-wing monoplanes similar to those being built in the West. The K-7 was a complete and stunning departure from what Kalinin had done before, and indeed from anything that had yet been attempted in the Soviet Union.

Because of its radical size and configuration, Kalinin had trouble selling it to the unimaginative planners in the Soviet government. The propaganda value helped, and so did Kalinin's promise to configure the first one as a *bomber*.

Work on the K-7 started in 1931, and the big airplane was completed two years later at Kalinin's design bureau plant in Kharkov. She was a true leviathan, built on a scale to rival Mother Russia herself. Her wingspan was 174 feet—equal to that of two DC-3s—and she was 92 feet long. Most notable about her size was her wing *area*. Kalinin had designed her with the largest elliptical wing that would ever be built. With an area of 4887 square feet, which was double that of a Boeing 314 Clipper or B-29, the huge wing was even greater in size than the wings of a B-52!

In what may well have been a concession to socialist egalitarianism, Kalinin's planners managed to find enough room in the K-7 to employ 19 people to crew the big ship. Within the wing, which was thick enough to accommodate 120 people, there were 12 separate crew positions, two each on either side of the engine nacelles. Seven of the crewmen were gunners, and could well have been put to work as stewards in an airliner variant if one had been forthcoming.

Powered by seven Soviet State Industries M34 engines delivering a total of 5810 hp, the K-7 was first flown on 11 August 1933. Violent vibrations shook the big tail booms, so huge slabs of steel were welded into place to keep them rigid, rather than looking into more subtle and complex aerodynamic solutions to the problem.

This also increased the K-7's 93,400 pound gross weight by 10 percent. Nevertheless, the test program managed to squeeze seven test flights out of the big elephant before 21 November, when the right tail boom wrenched off at 350 feet, sending the K-7 into a short, but deadly, power dive. Most of the small battalion of crewmembers were killed in the crash, and Kalinin found himself walking on eggshells for the rest of his life.

Konstantin Kalinin continued to develop other designs, but he was never to attempt anything on so grand a scale again. Two improved K-7s were requested, but were scrapped in 1935 before they were completed. Kalinin himself ran afoul of Josef Stalin's dreaded purges and was executed in 1938 as an enemy of the state.

Even before the K-7 was completed, the political advantage of gargantuan aircraft had caught fire in Stalin's workers' paradise.

In 1931, at the same time that Kalinin was embarking on his project, the Soviet government decided to build a huge airliner as a propaganda exercise in celebration of the great author Maxim Gorky.

It was Kalinin's idea, but it was being built without Kalinin. In fact it was a monumental committee effort that brought the best designers at the highly respected Tupolev design bureau together with virtual 'blank check' requisitioning power across the length and breadth of Soviet industry.

Built near Moscow in only nine months, the Ant-20 *Maksim Gorkii* was the largest airplane the world had ever seen when it was unveiled amid great fanfare in 1934. It had a wingspan of 206 feet 8 inches and was 108 feet long. The gross weight was 92,600 pounds. It was powered by six 900 hp M-34s in the wings and another two atop the fuselage. Inside it was like an ocean liner, very non-socialistic indeed.

The *Maksim Gorkii* could carry 72 passengers, with a select dozen of them assigned to sleeper suites. There was a bar and a buffet and a 16-line telephone interchange. There was a film processing lab and a small movie theater. If such amenities were not enough, Tupolev had also thrown in a laundry, a pharmacy and a *printing press*!

It first flew on 18 August 1934, and became an object of pride for the Soviet proletariat as it made demonstration flights over Moscow and other cities using huge public address speakers to make propaganda promulgations. Given conditions within the Soviet Union at the time, the use of such a grandiose platform to exhort the blessings of Stalin's regime was reminiscent of the excesses of an egomaniacal medieval despot. The big ship might have done some good for Stalin's international image had it undertaken a world tour, but it was never flown abroad.

The *Maksim Gorkii* had spent nearly a year of impressing the poor peasants when the end came on 18 May 1935. It was usually flown in the company of small single-engined aircraft to accentuate its size, and on this date, NP Blagin, in a Polikarpov I-5, attempted—on a whim—to loop the little biplane around the big aircraft. The maneuver failed as Blagin augered the I-5 into the *Maksim Gorkii*'s wing and the two went down, killing not only Blagin but the 10-person crew and 33 passengers aboard the big ship.

Public despair over the loss of the grand symbol was overwhelming and probably came a surprise even to Stalin. Millions of rubles were collected to build not one, but a whole fleet of replacements. Only one was built and it ultimately served not as a propaganda machine but as an Aeroflot liner on domestic routes. After the 1941 German invasion it was used as a rear area transport until being written off after a crash landing in December 1942.

Below: In a heavily retouched composite photograph, the Kalinin K-7 (bottom) and Tupolev Ant-20 are seen in formation flight. They were of the same ideal but were not contemporaries. The Soviet government may have liked Kalinin's idea, but poor Kalinin was executed as an enemy of the state.

The Brewster F2A Buffalo

At the start of World War II, most of the aircraft in the world's air forces were not, as one might expect, combat-proven. Some German and Soviet aircraft had done battle during the Spanish Civil War, but other than these and a few other exceptions, most warplanes were based solely on their designers' abstract calculations. In some cases—such as with the Supermarine Spitfire—these guesses proved to be exactly right, while in other instances the calculations were completely off the mark. The poor Brewster Buffalo was one of the latter.

Brewster Aircraft of Johnsonville, Pennsylvania was typical of the dark side of America's 'Arsenal of Democracy' during the Second World War. While the vast majority of the people in the United States industrial plant rolled up their sleeves and accomplished feats of efficiency and manufacturing output unparalleled in human history, there were the scoundrels, the profiteers, and the just plain befuddled. Some of these were investigated after the war, and some were simply overlooked or never uncovered. In the case of Brewster, management problems

got so bad that the US Navy had to walk into the factory in July 1944 and close the place down. That this was done at the height of the need for combat aircraft is certainly indicative of how badly things had deteriorated.

Brewster's first design for the Navy had been the FA-1 proposal in the mid-1930s that was in fact never built. The second was ordered in June 1936 under the XF2A-1 designation, and became the Navy's first monoplane fighter. On the surface it would have appeared to be a rather auspicious beginning, and indeed, Brewster *was* pioneering a new field. It was just that

Below: Thundering out of Bucks County, Pennsylvania, the Brewster F2A Buffalo both looked and flew like its namesake. During World War II, it took only three months for the Japanese to wipe out all of them.

Brewster didn't do a very good job. Because the world of monoplane fighters was in fact so new, the Buffalo's ineptitude wasn't immediately recognized.

The resulting aircraft was nearly 26 feet long with a wingspan of 35 feet and a painfully inadequate wing area. It weighed in at 2.5 tons, gross weight, and was powered by a Wright R-1820 radial engine delivering 750 hp at altitude. Armament consisted of two .50 caliber machine guns in the cowling and one in each wing.

The XF2A-1 Buffalo prototype first flew in January 1938, and 54 F2A-1 production models were ordered five months later. The first 11 of these were delivered in the summer of 1939 and were assigned to the fighter wing aboard the USS *Saratoga*. Within a matter of weeks, Europe had been plunged into World

War II, and a good many of the belligerent began knocking on the doors of American aircraft manufacturers as their need for warplanes was now outstripping domestic production.

Somehow, the Finns found their way to Bucks County, Pennsylvania, and somehow they managed to talk the US Navy out of 43 of the original F2A-1 series. Another 40 were purchased by the Belgians, and were completed in the spring of 1940. Before they could be shipped, however, Belgium fell to the German Blitzkrieg and the Belgian air force ceased to exist. Britain's Royal Air Force, itself in desperate need of fighter aircraft, was only too glad to pick up the order. It was only when these erstwhile Belgian Buffalos arrived in England that their shortcomings began to be apparent.

The Buffalo was a pudgy bird, this much was evident from first glance, but she was also overweight and underpowered, and she was very sluggish to handle because of her small wing area. Not only this, but her landing gear couldn't withstand the rigors of aircraft carrier landings.

Compared to the performance of the German Bf-109, or to the RAF's own Spitfires and Hurricanes, the Buffalo was very much outclassed. It was for this reason that the RAF banished its new acquisition to the garrisons at Singapore and Rangoon, where it was assumed they would ride out the war as a show of force, and not having to fire a shot.

Even as early as the autumn of 1939, the US Navy had sought to address the shortcomings of the Buffalo by commissioning Brewster to build another variant powered by a 900 hp Wright R-1820-40. There were 43 of these built as F2A-2 in 1940, and 108 as F2A-3 in 1941.

When war came to the Pacific in December 1941 the Buffalo had the distinction of being among the first Western fighters to face the dreaded Japanese Mitsubishi Zero. Not only did the British have more than 150 of them in Singapore, Malaya and Burma, but the Dutch had purchased over 30 for use in the defense of their Netherlands East Indies.

The first encounters came as a stunning surprise because Japanese aviation technology had been incorrectly assumed to be inferior to that of Britain, Germany and the United States. The Zero was one of the best fighters in the world and more than a match for the lumbering Buffalo, a plane around which it could literally run circles. The Zero was faster, lighter and much more maneuverable. The RAF had expected their duel with the Japanese to be a walkover. It was, but not in the form expected. Within three months of the start of the war, every Buffalo in the Far East had been lost, giving the ignoble Brewster the distinction of having handed the Japanese complete air superiority over Southeast Asia on a silver platter.

Because the F2A's landing gear had proved unsuitable for use on aircraft carriers, the only American Buffalos to see action were those F2As assigned to Marine Fighter Squadron VMF-221 on Midway. During the Battle of Midway in June 1942, VMF-221 suffered 13 losses out of 19 aircraft launched during an air battle that lasted less than half an hour. One of the pilots who survived recalled that any pilot sent up in a Buffalo in the future should be written off before he took off!

Those F2As that still existed after Midway were promptly replaced by Grumman F4F Wildcats. Brewster itself went on to build the SB2A Buccaneer (an equally clumsy scout bomber which the US Navy had the good sense to never send into combat), but within two years the company had gone the way of the RAF's fleet of Buffalos.

Left: A formation of US Navy F2A-2 Buffalos peels off in a 3 August 1942 photograph. The pudgy birds *could* fly, but no one would ever call them fast.

The Bell P-39 Airacobra

The P-39 was born of a noble desire to break new ground technologically, but it was destined to be remembered more as millstone than a milestone. Originally designed in 1937, the Airacobra was the first fighter produced in the United States to have the engine located behind the pilot, and a 37 mm cannon ahead of the pilot that fired through the propeller hub. The engine's driveshaft ran through the cockpit, between the pilot's feet, to the propeller in the nose. This put the pilot up high enough that the Airacobra became the first American fighter to have an automobile-like door on the side of the cockpit.

The Airacobra was supposed to have been built with a turbo-supercharged Allison V-1710-17, but shortly after the first flight tests in April 1939, the US Army Air Corps decided to save money by revising the specifications and ordering the production aircraft with a non-supercharged V-1710-37 instead. It was a fateful turning point, for this decision rendered the P-39 worthless at altitudes above 17,000 feet, and thus damned it to mediocrity. Because of this lack of power, the Airacobra was actually dangerous. The Air Corps pilots even had a song to summarize their feelings:

> Don't give me a P-39
> With an engine that's mounted behind.
> It will tumble and roll,
> And dig a big hole.
> Don't give me a P-39.

The automobile door added to the danger by making it difficult to bail out of a P-39 if it went into a spin, or if it did in fact 'tumble and roll.'

In terms of size, the P-39 was almost exactly the same size as a Curtiss P-40 and slightly smaller than a North American P-51. It was 30 feet 2 inches long with a wing span of 34 feet. The gross weight ranged between 7000 and 7700 pounds, depending on the model, making the Airacobra considerably lighter than a P-51, although this difference in weight was largely attributable to fuel capacity, and the P-51 had double the range of the P-39.

Above: A Bell P-39K Aircobra with Allison V-1710-63 engine photographed in 1944 before being delivered into the US Army Air Forces. *Below:* A Bell P-39C in prewar markings at a US Army Airfield circa 1941.

Despite these shortcomings, Bell delivered 9558 P-39s between January 1941 and August 1944, although by the latter date, Airacobras had been completely withdrawn from first line service with the US Army Air Forces in favor of P-51s. The fact that the P-39 was used at all was due to that when the United States entered World War II, there wasn't much of a choice. The P-39 and P-40 were really the best single-engine fighters that the USAAF had available in reasonable numbers. As a result, the Airacobra saw a good deal of service during 1942 in the South Pacific and North Africa. In the Pacific, the P-39 was found to be inferior to the Mitsubishi Zero that was the queen of the Imperial Japanese Army and Navy. Though the Airacobra was probably better than the aforementioned Brewster Buffalo, the Zero could outclimb it because of its lack of a supercharger and outturn it because of its weight.

In service in North Africa with both American and British forces, the P-39 found its niche in service as a ground attack aircraft because it was fast and heavily-armored and because low-level operations suited its engine. It was this characteristic that made the P-39 attractive to the Soviet Union. In its actions against the Germans, the Red Air Force was almost entirely subverted to the requirements of the Red Army. In other words, it existed to serve the tactical needs of the ground forces, and a durable ground attack aircraft was very much in demand. By procuring P-39s from the Americans via the Lend Lease pro-

gram, the Soviets could supplement domestic production, which was meager at best in 1942. Because it was Lend Lease, the Soviets also knew they wouldn't be billed for the airplanes until later, when they could ignore the invoice. Ultimately, *half* the entire Airacobra production wound up in service on the Eastern Front.

In the meantime, Bell developed a follow-on to the P-39 that sought to address some of the Airacobra's shortcomings. Designated P-63 by the USAAF, it was called King Cobra. The P-63 had a taller tail, a larger wing — its span was 38 feet 4 inches — and was 32 feet 8 inches long. A single P-63D was tested with a P-51-style bubble canopy instead of the automobile doors, but this innovation was never adopted.

The King Cobra was more heavily armed than its predecessor, and it used a more powerful version of the Allison V-1710 engine, which was, alas, still not supercharged. The P-63 had greater range than the P-39, but still it could not match the performance of the P-51 and other first-line USAAF fighters. As a result, only a handful of King Cobras were retained by the USAAF, while most of the production run — 2456 altogether — were delivered into the Red Air Force.

Right: In the dirt and grit of a wartime fighter field, shark-faced Airacobras, their 'auto-style' doors wide open, prepare to face the enemy. It may have looked fierce, but the Airacobra was more likely to strike fear in the hearts of its pilots. *Below:* A P-39Q with its engine panel door open.

Left: A well-worn TP-39Q. A dual-control trainer, the TP-39Q had a jury-rigged second cockpit. *Below:* Jay Harp's war surplus P-39L in civilian colors, as it appeared on the postwar air race circuit.

Above: A postscript to Bell's wartime career was the XP-77, which was conceived in 1941 as a fighter that could be produced quickly and inexpensively out of plywood. By the time the first two were built, however, mass production of full-size quality airplanes obviated the need for the 'quick and cheap' concept and the P-77 program was canceled.

The Blohm & Voss Bv-141

Although the firm is best known for building Germany's World War II flying boats, Blohm & Voss is most notorious for its profoundly eccentric Bv-141. It was precisely this eccentricity which doomed an otherwise operable and reportedly reliable airplane.

The story of the poor, deformed Bv-141 began in the late 1930s when the Luftwaffe was shopping for a light ground attack aircraft to supplement the Junkers Ju-87 Stuka, which was already in production. Focke Wulf proposed its Fw-189, while at Blohm & Voss, designer Richard Vogt came up with what is certainly the most unconventional design to be built during the World War II era. It was also probably the most asymmetrical airplane ever flown.

It would be intriguing to know what Vogt had in mind when he conceived her, as it would be interesting to know what charisma he must have brought into play in order to convince his employers to take such a design to the Reich Luftfahrtsministerium (Air Ministry). In any case, the RLM was predictably appalled by this strange contrivance and refused to appropriate a single pfenning for its production. There were scowls and snickering and suggestions that Blohm & Voss stick to flying boats. Focke Wulf's Fw-189 won the production contract.

Blohm & Voss was, however, sufficiently impressed with the Bv-141, that they actually undertook to build it at their own expense. The airplane that emerged from Vogt's drawings was remarkably aerodynamic, the fact of which he'd already known. It was 39 feet 10 inches long, with a wingspan of 50 feet 8 inches and a weight of 8600 pounds, putting it in almost exactly the same size and weight class as the familiar Messerschmitt Bf-110. Powered by a BMW132 865 hp radial engine, the Bv-141 had a respectable top speed of 248 mph and a ceiling of 29,530 feet, while its 700-mile range was almost *twice* that of the Fw-189.

Its first flight, on 25 February 1938, proved the Bv-141 to be more airworthy than its detractors wanted to believe. Over the next two years three prototypes and 10 Bv-141A production aircraft were completed, but the poor bird never shook the stigma of its disfigured appearance.

Below and right: Richard Vogt designed the BV-141 as though he were writing an engineering thesis. It worked, but pilots refused to trust such unorthodox lines and the British laughed at them.

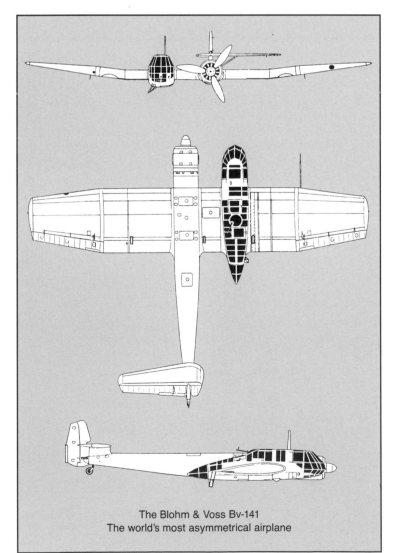

The Blohm & Voss Bv-141
The world's most asymmetrical airplane

The General Motors (Fisher Body Division) P-75 Eagle

The 'Fisher Eagle' was probably the most ill-conceived American airplane of World War II. At best, it was an airplane that almost nobody believed in. At worst, the whole program was a disgraceful prevarication. It was an airplane with which Dr William Christmas (see pages 44–47) would have been quite comfortable.

The story of the P-75 began in 1942, when General Oliver Echols, head of the USAAF Materiel Command, was putting together a giant, nationwide production consortium to build the B-29 Superfortress. The Boeing B-29 was to be the biggest strategic bomber ever put into production, and also one of the most complex. It was a weapons system of truly awesome proportion that had the capability of playing a vital role in winning the war for the Allies. Boeing had designed the B-29 and it could build *some* of them, but not as many as the USAAF wanted. Therefore, Echols wanted to bring other companies into

the program to help build additional B-29s. Bell and Martin were called upon, and actually would end up building a great many of the big bombers. That was all very well and good, but Echols *also* wanted General Motors' help.

General Echols had brought the Ford Motor Company into a similar consortium to build B-24 Liberators, but he *really* wanted GM involved in the B-29 project. At that time, GM was the biggest industrial company in the world, a vast complex with a proven track record in terms of both engineering expertise and the ability to manage truly massive manufacturing programs. The only problem was that GM felt that it was already too overcommitted to other war-related activities, and did not want in on the B-29 consortium. This being wartime, Echols had it within his power to *compel* the reluctant giant to do his bidding, and GM's Fisher Body Division plant in Cleveland, Ohio, was brought in as a B-29 manufacturing site. General Motors real-

ized that in order to get out of this commitment, they would have to come up with an *overriding* commitment. Thus it was that the 'Fisher Eagle' was born. In September 1942, GM went to Echols with the strange concoction that they hoped would get them out of having to build B-29s. The airplane that they proposed would be built around the V-3420-19 water-cooled engine (composed of two V-1710s in a side-by-side layout) that was already in production with GM's Allison Division.

Allison had plenty of practical experience with airplane engines, but Fisher had none with airplanes. To get around this slight obstacle, GM advanced a design which, in retrospect, is so preposterous that it is hard to believe that Echols bought it. It would be a peculiar hybrid with the wings of a Curtiss P-40, the landing gear of a Vought F4U, and the tail of a Douglas SBD dive bomber.

In a scenario that proves that truth is stranger than fiction, General Echols agreed to let GM go ahead with two prototypes that were assembled from body parts already produced for other airplanes. Produced under the designation XP-75, and promised by April 1943, the first Eagles were not ready to fly until November 1943. General FO Carroll, Chief of Engineering for the Materiel Command, noted three reasons for the delay: 'incompetent personnel at General Motors who requisitioned large amounts of government-furnished equipment compo-

nents, difficulty in handling required government-furnished equipment, and original [overly] optimistic estimates made by Fisher Body.'

When they did appear, the Eagles were 41 feet 6 inches long, with a wingspan of 49 feet 1 inch, and gross weight of 13,807 pounds. The engines, like that of a P-39, were located behind the pilot, driving two contra-rotating propellers via long shafts that ran through the cockpit.

The XP-75 left a great deal to be desired. It was sluggish to handle, with a poor roll rate, and it was incapable of the promised speed. A revised P-75A was developed, and delivered in early 1944, with the hope that it might satisfy the need for a long-range escort fighter, but this too fell far short of expectations. By this time, $4.3 million (including $1.5 million in cost overruns) had gone into funding the first eight Eagles.

The 'Fisher Eagle' program was terminated on 27 October 1944, after the completing of only six airplanes, and GM submitted a final bill for $4.7 million in May 1945. On one hand, the P-75 had been a $9 million, resource-consuming failure that was doomed from conception. On the other, it succeeded splendidly in its first and foremost purpose — it kept General Motors out of having to build B-29s!

Below: The P-75 'Fisher Eagle' was a hybrid and a miserable failure.

The Hughes F-11

To many people, the F-11 was the work of a madman. Indeed, this is the reputation which the enigmatic Howard Robard Hughes took to his grave. He was a billionaire when he died in 1976, and some said he was the richest man in the world. He was also a pathological recluse who hadn't been seen in public for two decades, and some said he was stark, raving mad.

In his early years, however, Hughes was a dashing and flamboyant character. He was born rich, but he accumulated most of his fortune himself. He consorted with movie stars, started his own film company and he married glamor-girl Jane Russell. His most lasting impact, however, was in aviation. He built airplanes, and he flew airplanes. In 1938 he set a world's speed record for a flight around the world in a Lockheed Model 14 Super Electra, and a year later—as owner of TransWorld Airlines—he was responsible for nudging Lockheed down the road that would lead to the Constellation, one of the two greatest piston-engined airliners in history.

It was the airplanes that Hughes built during World War II that are seen as his greatest failures, and the factors that may very well have sowed the seeds of his madness.

The plane which would ultimately evolve into the F-11 had its genesis in 1939 under the Hughes Aircraft experimental model designation DX-2. Hughes originally proposed it as a bomber, but the key element of his interest seems to have been the idea of constructing a large airplane by the Duramold process. This process had been developed and patented by Colonel Virginius E Clark, the Army's chief aeronautical engineer during the First World War. Duramold involved molding resin-impregnated plywood into desired shapes and contours under high heat and pressure. Pound for pound, it had been demonstrated that Duramold wooden structure had strength and rigidity comparable to metal.

In 1941, the United States was not yet involved in World War II, but the USAAF was in the midst of building up its strength in the expectation of that eventuality. Meanwhile, the DX-2 project had evolved into a large two-seat fighter design which interested the US Army Air Forces because aluminum was becoming scarce because of World War II. In October 1941, after officially scrutinizing the DX-2, the USAAF Materiel Command at Wright Field, Ohio, decided against the Hughes proposal because it couldn't quite a picture a future that involved something so archaic as *wooden* airplanes.

After the United States entered the war, USAAF headquarters in Washington urged the Materiel Command to reconsider the project. On 25 May 1942, the Hughes Duramold airplane was ordered under the experimental attack designation XA-37. Subsequently, the project was briefly considered for deployment as a night fighter under the experimental fighter designation XP-73. The eccentric Hughes, however, decided not to 'sell' the airplane to the USAAF until it made its first flight. This event transpired 11 months later, on 20 June 1943, with Howard Hughes at the controls. It was 43 feet long, with a wing span of 60 feet 5 inches (some sources say 66 feet), and a gross weight of 28,110 pounds. Power was supplied by two Pratt & Whitney R-2800 Double Wasp 2000 hp engines.

It was estimated to have had a top speed of 433 mph, but this is unknown, because Hughes himself was the only test pilot the airplane ever knew, and the only time someone was in the

Right: The second prototype Hughes F-11 during flight tests in 1948. Its predecessor crashed with Howard Hughes himself at the controls.

cockpit with Hughes during a high-speed test flight, the then-millionaire held his hand over the airspeed indicator!

The secrecy surrounding the development of the DX-2 exceeded that of a military program. All of the flying was done at a secret Hughes Aircraft facility at Harper's Dry Lake in the Mojave Desert, by Hughes himself. Furthermore, he wouldn't permit any photographs to be taken of the airplane.

The story of the Hughes DX-2 ended mysteriously on 11 November 1943 when a fire struck the hanger that contained the wooden aircraft, destroying both, along with any hope of the A-37 attack series ever coming into existence. Contemporary accounts speak of a lightning storm, while more recent recollections remember that the air was clear, and that the lightning came as a surprise. There were inevitable rumors of arson, but nothing was ever proven. There were fingers pointed at Howard Hughes, but it remains unclear what possible motive he would have had for destroying the mysterious airplane. In any case, the Materiel Command was noticeably relieved at not having to go through with buying any wooden A-37s.

In the meantime, Colonel Elliot Roosevelt, the son of the President and a friend of Hughes, had been lobbying in Washington on behalf of the project and had convinced USAAF chief General Henry H 'Hap' Arnold that a DX-2-based aircraft would make an ideal high altitude reconnaissance aircraft because of its potential speed and light weight. This line of

Below: The sleek Hughes F-11 might have revolutionized aerial reconnaissance if it hadn't been the centerpiece of a feud between an eccentric billionaire and a cantankerous Congress. After his battle with Congress, Howard Hughes would never build another plane.

thinking came as the USAAF had observed—and even used—the Royal Air Force's deHavilland Mosquito, a remarkable high altitude recon bird, that was made of *wood*. Hughes had even completed design studies for such an aircraft under his own D-5 designation.

Despite the continued reluctance of the Materiel Command, Hap Arnold compelled them to issue a purchase order offering in October 1943, to pay $56.6 million for 100 D-5s, which would be given the USAAF designation F-11. Ironically, the compromise was that the F-11 would be based on the design of the DX-2, but it would have to be *metal*, not wood.

It is worth noting here that the 'F' series of designations stood for 'photographic reconnaissance' prior to 1948, after which they were assigned to fighters, and the recon aircraft were given 'R for reconnaissance' prefixes. Also of importance here is that the F-11 was the first of the series to be designed from the *beginning* as a high performance reconnaissance aircraft. All the others—F-1 through F-10—were modified versions of some other type of aircraft.

The contract called for the F-11 to have a range of 5000 miles, with a top speed of 450 mph, and a first delivery date of March 1945. There were a great many teething problems inherent in the development of so unique a plane as the F-11, but the project was proceeding reasonably well, with the first prototype being 80 percent completed, until May 1944, when 21 Hughes engineers, including the F-11 project engineer, quit their jobs in a disagreement with their boss. From this point on, despite Hughes' promises to the contrary, the F-11 was continuously benighted by delays and chronic labor shortages. For example, the first set

of wings did not reach the Culver City, California, final production site from the subcontractor until 10 April 1945, a month after the scheduled first delivery of a completed airplane. The first of the two Pratt & Whitney R-4360 engines with their eight-bladed contra-rotating propellers wasn't available until September, the month the war ended.

In the meantime, on 26 May 1945, the USAAF had decided to cancel 98 of the 100 F-11s and pay Hughes $8.6 million to complete the first two. Howard Hughes was immensely displeased by this turn of events, and became obsessive about completion of the project as a means of demonstrating its validity to his detractors.

The first F-11 was ready for taxi tests by April 1946, and on 24 April, it was flown briefly at an altitude of 20 feet. It was a remarkably clean airplane. With a length of 65 feet 5 inches, and a wingspan of 101 feet 5 inches, the F-11 was nearly as big as a heavy bomber, yet it was as sleek and trim as a fighter.

Everything went well in the early tests, except for the potentially disastrous, and unexplainable, tendency for the propellers to change pitch without warning. Thus it was that the first flight was delayed until 7 July 1946.

Again, it was Howard Hughes himself at the controls. The first flight originated at Culver City and had lasted a bit more than an hour when loss of hydraulic fluid caused the rear part of the right propeller to reverse pitch, causing severe drag and loss of lift on the right side. Hughes tried to compensate for the problem by throttling back the left engine to balance the two. He attempted an emergency landing on the Los Angeles Country Club golf course, but it went down 300 feet short, crashing into the Beverly Hills-home of Lt Col Charles Meyer, who was away in Nuremberg, Germany, serving as an interpreter at the War Crimes Trials. Both house and airplane were completely destroyed.

Hughes suffered a broken leg, multiple lacerations and a possible skull fracture. He arrived at Beverly Hills Emergency Hospital still conscious, but was given only a 50-50 chance of survival. He would, in fact, live for another 30 years, but it can be said that he never recovered.

A USAAF accident board severely chastised Hughes for his handling of the flight—for everything from failure to use the proper radio frequencies to failing to feather the right prop at the first sign of trouble. A year later, in August 1947, Hughes found himself hauled up before the Senate War Investigating Committee on charges that he and Elliot Roosevelt had used undue political influence to advance two airplanes—the F-11 and the HK-1—that many now considered to have been expensive failures. Roosevelt countered by charging the Materiel Command with collusion with larger airplane builders in an effort to 'freeze out' smaller planemakers like Hughes.

The 1947 Senate hearings ended with findings of neither fraud nor collusion. A second F-11 was completed in November 1947 and flight tested in 1948 with conventional propellers. A third F-11 was reportedly under construction, but it was apparently never completed. The test program ended quietly with the multi-million dollar political football left parked on the grounds of Shepard AFB in Texas. Howard Hughes would never build another airplane, but the F-11 and the HK-1 remain well placed in the pantheon of aviation idiosyncracies.

The Messerschmitt
Me-321/Me-323 Gigant

Dr Willy Messerschmitt must certainly be remembered as one of the world's greatest aircraft designers. Messerschmitt is remembered for his immortal Bf-109 fighter, for the Me-262, the world's first jet fighter, and for several other of the Luftwaffe's best warplanes. His aircraft were on the leading edge of aviation technology, both at the start and finish of World War II, and during the war, they constituted the backbone of German airpower.

However, the desperate urgencies of war make men take reckless chances. If such gambles work out, he's a genius, but if they don't, history remembers a fool. While we hardly remember Messerschmitt as a fool, the Me-321/Me-323 program was clearly foolhardy, and hardly worth the precious resources that were poured into it. Responsibility—or might we say blame—for the project lies both with Luftwaffe chief Reichsmarschal Herman Goering and with Dr Messerschmitt himself. Both of them had more than simply a professional interest in the concept and in the project that it begat.

It all began in October 1940, at a time when Operation Sea Lion (the German invasion of Britain) had been postponed until the spring of 1941. As part of the invasion effort, Goering wanted to develop means of airlifting tanks and other heavy equipment across the English Channel so that they would be available for immediate use by the first airborne troops to land in Britain. The concept then under study held that the best and most expedient way to accomplish the task was to use a *disposable* glider for the task. The aircraft would essentially be designed for a short one-way flight across the channel, and thus certain shortcuts could be taken in its construction. A sketch in Willy Messerschmitt's own hand that is still preserved at the Imperial War Museum in London shows a Panzer Mk3 tank with wings, fuselage and tail attached, being towed by four Junkers Ju-52 transports.

The German Air Ministry put the project out to bid by various firms and, ironically, Messerschmitt lost the first round of the competition for the contract to Junkers. However, when a tank crashed through the flimsy wooden floor of the Junkers Ju-322

The Messerschmitt Me-321 glider *(below)* proved impractical so it became the vulnerable six-engine Me-323 *(right)*.

Mammut (Mammoth), Goering turned to Messerschmitt. Already, however, the entire project was taking on an almost slapstick undertone.

Built under the designation Me-321, the big Messerschmitt glider was completed in short order. By March 1941 it rolled out of the factory at Leipheim, ready for its first test flight. Named Gigant (Giant), it was a true behemoth. It was 92 feet 4 inches long, with a wingspan of 180 feet 5.5 inches, larger than any of the world's strategic bombers, and larger than any transport then in routine service. It had a gross weight of 75,900 pounds and a cargo capacity of 22 tons, enough to accommodate a light tank. Huge, clamshell doors in the nose were an innovation that permitted the loading of oversize cargo.

The project specifications had evolved beyond the days of the disposable glider, but this concept still clouded the thinking of the people working on the Gigant. She was lightly built of fabric stretched over a metal framework, and she was aerodynamically sound. After all, Willy Messerschmitt had been designing gliders since he was a teenager. The problem was that no one had ever flown a glider this big before. She took to the air nicely, but the huge control surfaces were so large that the pilot had to struggle to manage the big monster. Problems were also encountered in trying to find an aircraft big enough to tow the Gigant. A Ju-90 airliner that was used on the initial flight tests proved inadequate, so a trio of Bf-110 fighters was employed in a triangular 'troika-schlepp' formation, with mixed results. The best, albeit cumbersome, solution was found to be in the creation of the Heinkel He-111Z Zwilling, which was actually two He-111s bolted together side-by-side. The Luftwaffe also experimented with rocket-assisted takeoff, using a battery of small Walter 109 rockets in various configurations.

Despite the problems, the Me-321 went into production immediately. Three individual Luftwaffe transport squadrons were organized to receive them and 175 were completed by April 1942. When Sea Lion was finally cancelled in 1941, the Me-321 fleet was assigned to the Eastern Front, where transport of any sort was very much in need.

Meanwhile, Messerschmitt's engineers had begun work on what seems, in retrospect, to be an obvious step in the evolution of this ill-conceived elephant. This involved fitting the Gigant with engines of its own. The proposal called for drawing upon a large stockpile of pre-existing Gnome-Rhone 14N radial engines that had been captured after the fall of France in 1940.

Originally designated Me-321C, the first of the powered Gigants was completed early in 1942 under the designation Me-323C. The four-motored Me-323 was quickly abandoned in favor of a six-motored Me-323D, which was ordered into production. The Me-323 had the same overall dimensions as the unpowered version, but the six 1140 hp engines gave it a 26 percent increase in gross weight. This extra load-carrying capacity looked good on paper, but, with a top speed of only 177 mph, the cumbersome monster could fly at only half the speed of Allied interceptors. Attempts to get 1600 hp BMW801 engines were circumvented due to prior commitment of these engines to other projects.

The first Me-323 squadron entered service in October on the Mediterranean Front. This was the first mistake. Gigants had heretofore survived on the Eastern Front because of the Luftwaffe's unquestioned air superiority. In the Mediterranean, the Luftwaffe was constantly at odds with the equally—and soon to be more—potent Royal Air Force and US Army Air Forces.

Right: Loading sturdy Wehrmacht Cavalry horses aboard an Me-323 somewhere on the Eastern Front. The clamshell doors permitted loading of a variety of large objects.

A good illustration of how disastrous the deployment of Me-323s to the Mediterranean really was came on 22 April 1943. General Erwin Rommel's Afrika Korps, undermanned and undersupplied, had been fighting a brilliant holding action against the Anglo-American forces, but they were now cornered in Tunisia and running desperately low on everything. After having ignored Rommel's pleas for months, the German high command now realized that the entire North African Front would be lost if he were not supplied en masse immediately.

Two transport squadrons with 16 Gigants were pressed into service with their nearly 300 tons of lifting capacity. Again it looked good on paper. It was a bold and masterful stroke that would revive both the stomachs and the morale of Rommel's war-weary troops. The only problem was the RAF. Loaded to the gills, the Gigants were transformed from transports to targets. They were slow and utterly unmaneuverable. They were literally sitting ducks.

When 22 April 1943 came to an end, only two of the Me-323s had reached Tunis. The remaining 14 had been shot down. Further attempts to use the Gigants to supply the Afrika Korps also ended in disaster, and a month later, the remaining aircraft were transferred to the Eastern Front, where the Luftwaffe still had some measure of air superiority. In Russia the Gigants played a role in the German efforts to hold Stalingrad, but their fragility more than offset the value of their large payload potential.

Production of the Me-323 ended in March 1944 with 201 units, and the last of those which was not lost to enemy action or technical strife was withdrawn from service three months later. The big cow of an aircraft had been conceived of questionable logic and kept in service much longer than it should have. What had been demonstrated was the desirability of heavy airlift capacity. The pitifully slow and unwieldy Gigant had the capacity, but it had virtually nothing to offer in the way of reliability.

Below and right: The huge and clumsy Messerschmitt Me-323 Gigant.

The Mitsubishi G4M 'Betty'

Produced in larger numbers (2416) than any other Japanese bomber during World War II, the G4M saw service throughout the Pacific and its career spanned the entire conflict. G4Ms helped sink the HMS *Repulse* and the HMS *Prince of Wales* two days after Pearl Harbor in 1941, and a G4M carried the Japanese delegation to surrender in 1945. In between, the aircraft's great range made it an extremely useful weapon, especially in Southeast Asia. There was only one drawback: the huge, unprotected fuel tanks were prone to catch fire easily, turning the G4M into a torch. The tanks had to be big, and the airplane unarmored to achieve a maximum range of 3765 miles, but the lack of protection was deadly.

Known to its crews as the 'flying cigar,' or the 'flying lighter,' the G4M more than held her own in the early days of the war, but revealed her terrible vulnerability when subjected to the abuse of Allied fighter aircraft, which became a serious threat after 1942. During one raid on Port Moresby in January 1943, 10 out of 17 G4Ms failed to return.

Officially called Rikujoh Kohgekiki (Land-based Bomber),

the G4M was assigned the Allied code name Betty, a misleading appellation for an aircraft that was so unforgiving to friend and foe alike. Betty was 65 feet 7 inches long with a wing span of 82 feet and a gross weight of 33,000 pounds, making it about a fifth bigger than its twin-engined American counterparts the North American B-25 and Martin B-26.

The G4M continued to be used as a bomber throughout the war, and in 1945 was also used to carry the infamous Ohka manned Kamikaze rocket (*see below*). In both roles, however, it had become almost as much of suicide plane as the Ohka. In the face of the stiff fighter opposition that it faced—especially in the last two years of the war—the G4M was an example of an aircraft that was more dangerous to its own crews than it was to the enemy. This grim reality was made doubly despicable by the fact that the Japanese Imperial Navy had no adequate substitute, and continued building and deploying G4Ms until the bitter end.

Right: A G4M carrying an MXY7 Ohka flying bomb. *Below:* A 'Betty' at Mizutani, Japan, with her props removed prior to the September 1945 surrender.

The Yokosuka MXY7 Ohka

It was one of the most grisly machines ever designed—an airplane that existed to kill its own pilot. In 1944, as the Japanese Empire was sensing the end, the fanatic samurai who ruled the code by which the Japanese fighting man lived and died, concocted the ruthless doctrine of Kamikaze (Divine Wind), which literally involved pilots crashing their airplanes into American ships.

The Kamikaze attacks were first encountered during efforts to recapture the Philippines in July 1944, and reached their crescendo during the invasion of Okinawa in April 1945. They would have been the first line of defense against the Allied invasion of Japan itself, but the war ended before this invasion became necessary.

Initially the Kamikaze attacks were conducted in aircraft originally designed for other purposes—fighters, bombers and even rickety biplane trainers. The doctrine reached a new level of madness, however, in April 1945, when the Yokosuka MXY7 Ohka (Cherry Blossom) made its ghastly debut at Okinawa.

The Ohka was essentially a rocket-propelled flying torpedo with 2646 pounds of high explosive in the nose and a human being to guide it into the target. Ironically, this desperate creation was the only non-propeller driven aircraft to see widespread service with Japanese forces during World War II. It was 19 feet 11 inches long, with a wingspan of 16 feet 9 inches. The gross weight was 4700 pounds, with over half of that being the explosive warhead. The powerplant was a cluster of three Type 4 short duration (three to four minutes) rockets, delivering 1760 pounds of thrust. In its final moments—which consisted of a steep dive from which it was neither designed, nor intended, to recover—the Ohka could reach speeds of nearly 600 mph. This made it particularly deadly to Allied shipping, and very hard to shoot down.

Designed at the Imperial Navy's big Yokosuka complex on Tokyo Bay during the summer of 1944, the Ohka was built by a variety of Japanese manufacturers, including Dai Ichi Kaigun, and the firms of Fuji and Hitachi, whose products—albeit of a different nature—are still familiar to consumers today.

Of the total of 852 Ohkas that were built, 755 were of the Model 11 type seen here. Other variants included the jet propelled Model 22, which had a longer range and which carried a 1320-pound bomb in addition to its internal payload. The most ghoulish version was probably the Model 43, which was essentially a training form of the Model 11 with the warhead replaced by a second cockpit, and with a landing skid so that this craft—unlike the Model 11—could be recovered. One wonders what must have gone through the minds of the people who trained others to fly the Ohka.

A typical Ohka mission began with the pilot being bolted into the cockpit sans parachute and airlifted to within roughly 20 miles of its target by a carrier plane, which was usually a Mitsubishi G4M such as is seen on pages 79 and 82–83. It was thus carried because the MXY7's engines and simple aerody-namic design did not permit it to take off from a runway under its own power. Furthermore, except for the handful of Model 43 trainers, the Ohkas were incapable of landing.

After being released from the carrier plane, the pilot would start the engines and have three to four minutes to find his target, which was usually American shipping. The Americans called the Ohkas 'Baka Bombs' (Fool Bombs), and they were as deadly as they were insane. In their first deployment, off Okinawa on 1 April 1945, an Ohka hit and severely damaged the battleship USS *West Virginia* (BB-48), a survivor of Pearl Harbor. On 12 April, an Ohka was responsible for its type's first ship sunk, as the destroyer USS *Mannert L Abele* (DD-733) went down off Okinawa.

The Ohka was a macabre act of desperation, but it failed to effect the war's final outcome. Indeed, it is hard to imagine a society that could consciously design, build and deploy a weapon such as the Ohka, but in war, mankind is driven to some rather barbaric ends.

Below: An MXY7 on display in the United States after the war.

Above: A Mitsubishi G4M 'Betty' releases a Yokosuka MXY7 Ohka against the American Fleet in April 1945. The G4M was a dangerous aircraft when attacked because it caught fire easily. The Ohka was especially ugly because it was designed to kill its own pilot in a Saturnian rite of self-inflicted death for the glory of a soft-spoken emperor who would outlive the Ohka pilots by 44 years.

The Ohka was also deadly for the Americans who were its target because it was virtually unstoppable.

The Bachem Ba-349 Natter

By the beginning of 1944, Germany was the acknowledged world leader in advanced jet- and rocket-powered aircraft. The only problem seemed to be that the Luftwaffe high command and the Fuhrer himself were decidedly ambivalent to the fact. By the end of the year, when the upper echelons of the German power structure realized the nature and importance of this tremendous resource, it was too late — World War II was all but lost.

From Adolf Hitler on down, the cry went out for 'secret weapons' to stun the Allies and win the war. Had this call been made in 1942, it would have been technologically possible for Germany to have achieved in 1944 what it took the rest of the world until 1954 to achieve. As it was, only the remarkable Messerschmitt Me-262 jet fighter was ever produced in sufficient numbers to have a real impact during the air war. Nevertheless, at least a half dozen other jet- and rocket-powered aircraft were built and tested, and some, such as the Messerschmitt Me-163 Komet and the Arado Ar-234 Blitz, actually were used in combat. There were also literally hundreds of others on the drawing board, or in various stages of construction, when the war ended in May 1945.

Some of the German jet and rocket warplanes were the result of many years of careful calculations, while others were almost hysterical monsters brought to life by convulsions of sheer desperation. The Bachem Ba-349 was one of the latter.

Nicknamed Natter (Adder), the Ba-349 was designed as a target-defense interceptor, a simple, yet very fast, aircraft that could be pre-positioned near potential targets of Allied bombers and launched at a moment's notice. It was 18 feet 9 inches long, with straight, stubby wings measuring 11 feet 10 inches from tip to tip. Built primarily of wood and other non-crucial materials, the Ba-349 weighed 5000 pounds fully fueled. It was designed to be launched vertically, thus eliminating the need for an airfield and permitting it to be stationed virtually anywhere.

In the operational scenario, Natters would be launched as Allied bombers neared the target. A single Walter HWK109 rocket motor, delivering up to 4410 pounds of thrust, would kick the aircraft up to 29,000 feet in less than a minute. The aircraft

would be under the control of ground-based radar operators until contact was made with the enemy, whereupon the pilot would assume control, jettison the nose cap and begin attacking the bomber formation with two dozen 73 mm Foehn (or 33 R4M 55 mm) unguided rockets. Seven minutes after reaching altitude, the fuel would be expended and the pilot would save himself and the motor, using a primitive ejection system.

The remarkable thing about the Ba-349 was that it went from initial conception to first test flight in only six months. Conceived in August 1944, two months after the invasion of France, the first Natter was hoisted into its launch tower on 28 February 1945. Before the day was out, that Ba-349 and its precious rocket motor were spread in pieces across the German countryside and test pilot Lothar Siebert was the program's first martyr.

Within two months, the Ba-349 had actually been successfully flown and a pilot recovered. Also by April 1945, a staffel (squadron) of 10 had been put into position near Kirchheim. None of these was ever flown operationally, however, and the entire site was purposely destroyed to keep the aircraft from falling into American hands, although at least one Bachem Viper was taken intact. In the end, the hastily conceived and constructed Bachem death trap cost more Luftwaffe lives than it did those of Allied flyers.

Facing page: The prototype Bachem Ba-349 on its launch tower in February 1945. A few days later, the initial launch attempt turned grisly. Test pilot Lothar Siebert never knew what hit him. *Above:* A good view of a Natter strapped and palleted for shipment. Note the 24 Foehn aerial rockets packed into its nose, and the crude aiming device. *Below:* One of the Natters (aka 'Viper') captured by the US Army at Kirchheim near Stuttgart was shipped back to the States for public display. *Overleaf:* The Bachem Natter was fairly crude, as befits an aircraft that was designed to be used once and discarded. It was the world's first disposable aircraft.

The Douglas XSB2D-1 'Turkey'

The Douglas SBD (Scout Bomber, Douglas) Dauntless was probably the most notable attack bomber in the arsenal of the US Navy's carrier force during World War II. The SBD, however, represented prewar technology, and the war had barely begun when the Navy asked Douglas to begin thinking about a successor which would be designated as XSB2D-1 (Scout Bomber, Second, Douglas).

The Navy specifications called for a tricycle landing gear, two remotely controlled gun turrets and a great many other innovations. Ed Heinemann, the ace designer, who had designed the Dauntless—and who would design most of the great Douglas postwar combat aircraft—remembered that 'contemplation of these requisites was discomforting. We were complicating the

machine. It loomed in sharp contrast to the image of a simplified, functionally designed aircraft which the flyers could handle and the maintenance men support with reasonable ease.'

The XSB2D-1 would also have to carry its bomb load internally, rather than on external racks like the SBD. This meant that the landing gear would have to retract into the wing, and that the wing would have to be thicker—and heavier. Size was also a problem because the finished aircraft would have to fit into the fixed size of aircraft carrier elevators. Gull wings were adopted as a compromise to permit shorter landing gear, and so save a precious few inches.

The first of two XSB2D-1s was first flown on 8 April 1943, with pilot LaVerne 'Tailspin Tommy' Brown (the former Holly-

wood stunt flyer) calling it 'nothing to write home about.'

The new aircraft was 38 feet 7 inches long, with a wingspan of 45 feet. As such, she was only about 10 percent larger than the SBD, but, because of all the extras that the Navy had required, she had a gross weight of 16,273 pounds, which was more than double that of the Dauntless, and 2500 pounds greater than the Navy's own specifications for the XSB2D-1. After completion of the second prototype in 1944, the entire program was cancelled.

She was an airplane that no one, neither customer nor designer, could love. Wrote Ed Heinemann: 'Although it demonstrated reasonably good high-speed characteristics, we were instinctively aware that we didn't have an overwhelming winner on our hands . . . . We learned a bitter lesson. If the plane was not a failure, it was most certainly, in today's vernacular, a turkey.'

Right: The Douglas SBD Dauntless, one of the most important aircraft in naval history. *Below:* Even its own designer described the XSB2D-1 as a 'turkey.'

The Douglas BTD-1 Destroyer

Even before the XSB2D-1 program was cancelled, the US Navy was anxious to have Douglas begin work on a torpedo bomber that would utilize whatever lessons could be gleaned from the previous program. The result was the BTD-1 (Scout Bomber, Torpedo, Douglas) Destroyer, an aircraft which had the same dimensions as the XSB2D-1, as well as the same type of Wright R3350 radial engine. However, the new plane was much streamlined, and free of much of the complicating hardware, such as the gun turrets and second crew position. On the other hand, the BTD-1 weighed a ton more than the earlier 'turkey,' and had inferior performance.

The Destroyer was simply a compromised version of another airplane which had itself been a compromise. She first flew on 5 March 1944, but she never reached combat, and only 28 aircraft had been built by the time the war ended in 1945.

Like the XSB2D-1 before her, the BTD-1 lived and died without any enthusiastic support from anyone. Ed Heinemann, the man who wrenched both from the quagmire of byzantine Navy specifications, recalls the day in the sweaty, muggy heat of Washington, DC's summer of 1943, when he stood up in a meeting at the Navy's Bureau of Aeronautics and asked that the BTD-1 be cancelled.

Below: The Douglas BTD-1 program was an effort to make the XSB2D-1 concept workable. It was, in a sense, an attempt to effect a compromise upon a concept that had itself been reached by compromise. The BTD-1 had no real advocates either at Douglas or within the Navy Department and, in the end, Ed Heinemann himself asked the Navy's Bureau of Aeronautics to scrap the whole idea.

The Douglas XTB2D-1 Skypirate

Ordered by the US Navy in October 1943, the Skypirate represented the third in a triumvirate of 'turkeys' that were to the Navy's efforts to win World War II what airplanes like the GAX and GA-2 had been to the US Army's efforts to build a modern force after World War I. These were airplanes that looked good on the paper that brought them forth from government bureaucracy, but which represented so much committee-pleasing compromise that they were destined to mediocrity.

The XTB2D-1 (Torpedo Bomber, Second, Douglas) was half again larger than the XSB2D-1 or BTD-1. It was 46 feet long, with a wingspan of 70 feet and a gross weight of 28,545. At the time it was first flown in March 1945, it was too big to operate from any aircraft carrier in the US fleet. It had been deliberately designed to serve aboard the big, new *Midway*-class carriers that were then under construction in anticipation of the final attack on Japan. Laid down in 1943, and launched in March and April 1945 respectively, the USS *Midway* (CV-41) and USS *Franklin D Roosevelt* (CV-42) were commissioned within a few weeks of the end of World War II, but had the war continued,

they would have played a flagship role in the final invasion of Japan, Operation Coronet, scheduled for March 1946.

As it was, these big carriers served for many years, and during the course of two succeeding wars. While naval ship-building art reached an apogee during 1943-1945, the same was not true of aviation technology. The aircraft designed for these huge carriers in 1943 were barely state of the art when the ships were launched, and soon were clearly outclassed by fast high-performance jets.

The XTB2D-1 was one of the many aircraft that fell through the cracks. It was too big and too ambitious for its time, and obsolescent soon thereafter. Its 8000 pound bomb load (or two torpedoes) would have made it a good plane to operate from land bases in 1942, but by 1945, the same job could be handled by other aircraft, and just as efficiently by other, smaller, carrier planes. In retrospect, the true worth of the Skypirate was the role it played in paving the way for the BT2D (later AD) Skyraider, which would eventually be remembered as one of the greatest attack planes that Douglas ever built for the Navy.

Above and below: The Douglas XTB2D-1 Skypirate was an ambitious aircraft that wound up too big to operate from any World War II US Navy carriers.

The Douglas XA2D Skyshark

The great Douglas Skyraider, which first appeared in March 1945, went on to prove itself, in both Korea and Vietnam, as a highly capable and reliable warplane. Originally designated as BT2D for Scout Bomber, Torpedo, Second, Douglas, it was redesignated in 1946 as AD. The AD stood for Attack, Douglas, but her crews always interpreted it as 'Able Dog,' a term of affection that easily summarizes its career.

The Skyraider, like all US Navy aircraft before it, was powered by a piston engine. In the years immediately after World War II, there was a great deal of attention being focussed on the development of both turbojet and turboprop powerplants. They were appealing engines for use on carrier planes because of their inherent power and rapid acceleration. Thus it was, that as soon as the Navy realized that the Skyraider was going to be a winner, they asked Douglas to undertake development of a parallel, *turboprop* attack bomber. Remembering their lack of success with the three Navy-initiated bomber projects described above, Douglas was reluctant to present a design. Nevertheless, it was presented, and in September 1947, the Navy ordered two prototypes under the designation XA2D (Attack, Second, Douglas, Experimental prototype).

Dubbed Skyshark because of its pointed, sharklike nose, the XA2D-1 was 41 feet 4 inches long, slightly longer than a Skyraider, with a wingspan of 50 feet, identical to that of a Skyraider. It had a gross weight of 22,966 pounds, much heavier than most wartime carrier-based bombers, and heavier than most Skyraider variants. The Skyshark was powered by an experimental Allison XT40 turboprop that promised 5035 hp, double that of the Skyraider's Wright radial. It was this engine that was to be the Skyshark's downfall.

First there were the delays that the program suffered as General Motors' Allison Division struggled with the teething troubles suffered by the XT40. Next there was the difficulty in developing the complex set of gears necessary to drive the contra-rotating propellers. These challenges cost the program about a year's time, and the first flight didn't take place until 26 May 1950. With the start of the Korean War only a month later, the Navy quickly added orders for 341 A2Ds to the two XA2D prototypes already on the books.

The Douglas XA2D Skyshark with wings folded *(left)* and extended *(above).*

Above and opposite: The first Skyshark on a test flight over the Mojave Desert.

On 14 December 1950, however, the program was struck by the first of the disasters that would ultimately destroy it. Douglas test pilot Hugh Wood was at 20,000 feet over Edwards AFB on an XA2D test flight when one of the dual power units within the XT40 failed, ramming all the power from the prop back into the other unit. The Skyshark sank like a stone. Wood tried to make an emergency landing, but he was coming down so fast that when he hit the runway, the landing gear was rammed through the top of the wings.

Hugh Wood was killed, and the second prototype was delayed from making its first flight until 3 April 1952, but the program pushed forward. As Ed Heinemann recalled, the problems with the engine and gearbox were 'like a chronic toothache.'

There had been so much new and untried technology present in building and gearing the XT40, that a quick fix was impossible, and all attempts at a quick fix simply exacerbated an already overwhelming problem. Time slipped away like sea sand between one's fingers, and the Korean conflict ended without the Skyshark being *close* to production-ready.

In June 1953, Douglas test pilot CG 'Doc' Livingston was pulling out of a dive when both of the propellers literally wrenched out of the nose of the airplane, taking a large part of

the complex gearbox with them. Livingston didn't know what had happened at first because the canopy had been completely drenched with oil. Miraculously, he not only survived, but managed to set the disabled plane down, its turboprop engine still thundering mightily, but driving nothing.

Soon after, a gearbox failure nearly cost the life of Douglas test pilot George Jansen, and in September 1953, the program was terminated with but five of the 341 Skysharks having been delivered.

The repeated attempts to keep the Skyshark on track had been valiant at first, but they soon became ridiculous in the face of overwhelming odds. If there was ever an American airplane program that was truly beset by a 'jinx' or a gremlin, it was that of the XA2D, and more specifically the XT40 engine and gearbox. Clearly, the only solution was to trash the entire power system and start over, but by the time the program had gotten around to this, the Korean War—and the *need* for the production A2Ds—was over, and the Navy had already started taking delivery of *jet* attack bombers, notably one of the best: Ed Heinemann's Hot Rod, the Douglas A4D Skyhawk.

Below: A jinxed bird, the Douglas XA2D Skyshark was the victim of a gearbox that was so complex that it never could be made to work reliably. The XT-40 turboprop dual power units were also the source of disappointing and disastrous failures. In one test flight, the forward of the contra-rotating propellers literally wrenched itself off the airplane.

The Hughes-Kaiser HK-1 (H-4) Hercules (The *Spruce Goose*)

Just as Howard Hughes is synonymous with eccentricity, his notorious *Spruce Goose* has become synonymous with folly. The idea began in the dark days of 1942 when Allied shipping in the North Atlantic was being blasted with merciless efficiency by German U-boats. In discussing the situation, Hughes and shipping Tycoon Henry J Kaiser conceived the idea of a fleet of enormous flying boats that could obviate the U-boat threat by simply flying over it!

The airplane they envisioned would carry a greater payload than any aircraft ever imagined. It could transport hundreds of troops, full-size tanks and over 50 tons of cargo.

In September 1942, convinced that no airplane this large could possibly get into the air, the Joint Chiefs of Staff refused to approve the project, so Henry J Kaiser went directly to President Roosevelt's chief of staff, Admiral William Leahy, and walked away with an $18 million contract to build three prototypes. The

only problem was that the funding was contingent on finding a way to build the airplanes without the use of 'strategic materials.' In layman's terms—no aluminum.

For Hughes, who was a convert to the Duramold process of using resin-impregnated wood in aircraft production (see page 68), this was not a problem. Selecting the proper lumber, however, became obsessive and time consuming, as engineers employed by the Hughes-Kaiser joint venture roamed the forests

Above: Howard Robard Hughes, the eccentric billionaire, captured headlines with a record-setting 1938 round-the-world flight and went on to build the world's largest amphibian *(right and top right)*. *At right* we see the Spruce Goose en route to her final display building on Long Beach Harbor.

of the United States and Canada literally picking specific trees for specific parts of the huge first prototype. Though she would come to wear the nickname *Spruce Goose*—an appellation that Howard Hughes despised—the big prototype was constructed primarily of birch, with very little spruce present among her ingredients.

By the end of 1942, the worst of the U-boat threat had passed, but the HK-1 project had only just begun. The project stretched through 1943, and by February 1944, $13 million had been spent with Hughes-Kaiser having failed to complete even a single HK-1. In March, the government decided that completion of the project was no longer necessary to the war effort. (Many felt that it *never* was.) Completion of the prototype could go ahead under terms of the original contract, but the additional aircraft were cancelled and the government said it would not accept delivery of the single HK-1 until 1948.

In June 1946, nearly a year after the end of the war, the HK-1 Hercules was completed at Culver City, California and moved 28 miles to a specially constructed hanger on the edge of Long Beach Harbor. The move took two days and cost $80,000. The airplane itself had cost $25 million. When the government's $18 million ran out, Howard Hughes shoveled in $7 million from his own pocket to finish it.

It wasn't just the price tag that was enormous. Everything about the HK-1 Hercules was gargantuan. It was 218.5 feet long, as much as two B-29s, and only 13 feet shorter than a 747 jumbo jet of today. Its wing span was 320.5 feet, more than that of *three* Flying Fortresses, and more than half again greater than that of a 747. Even its tail, which was 113.5 feet across, was bigger than the wingspan of a B 17. Its 200-ton gross weight helped to convince its detractors that the Hercules was unflyable.

The HK-1 had been sitting in its Long Beach hanger for a little more than a year when Senator Owen Brewster called Howard Hughes before the Senate War Investigating Committee in August 1947 to accuse him of fraud and to call the HK-1 a 'lumberyard,' a 'white elephant' and worse. Hughes managed to successfully survive the hearings by winning public support with his admonishment to the senators that 'during the war, I got less than one percent of the aircraft contracts, and now I'm getting 99 percent of the investigations.'

The Senate backed off, but Hughes still had a 200-ton albatross around his neck, so he returned to Long Beach, ostensibly to take the HK-1 out for taxi trials. On Sunday, 2 November 1947, with 50,000 people watching, he taxied the birchwood behemoth onto the choppy waters of Long Beach Harbor. He ran up the eight Pratt & Whitney R-4360s and made several turns across the harbor, telling the 30 reporters who were aboard that the first flight would come in 1948. Then he dropped off the reporters and taxied out for one more test. Co-pilot Dave Grant lowered the flaps, Hughes throttled the engines up to 75 mph, and the HK-1 was airborne.

The flight lasted only 60 seconds, but it proved that the 'white elephant' could fly.

The world's largest airplane had finally flown, albeit five years after it was so desperately needed in the war's bleakest moments. She had cost Howard Hughes $117,000 for each second of her flight time, and she had cost the American taxpayers more than $300,000 for each of those seconds. It was more money in constant dollar terms than it would take to put a man on the moon.

The HK-1 was a remarkable novelty, but it was little more than this and a monument to obsolete technology. She was born in an era when gargantuan flying boats were seen as the wave of the future, but by the time she first flew, the idea was a thing of the past.

The plane now known as the *Spruce Goose* went back into her climate controlled hanger, where she would remain for the next 33 years. Howard Hughes commanded that she be kept constantly flight-ready, and she was, but their second flight would never come.

Above: Building the Hercules was something akin to building a ship, and indeed Henry J Kaiser was doing just that at the time. Although the vessels of Kaiser's vast armada of 'Liberty Ships' were smaller than the HK-1, the flying boat had a hull larger than those of most nineteenth century clipper ships.

Left: On 2 November 1947, when Howard Hughes himself took the HK-1 out for taxi trials on Long Beach harbor, nobody—probably not even Hughes—had any idea that he would take her up.

The McDonnell XF-85 Goblin

During the strategic air offensive against Germany during World War II, the US Army Air Forces had faced serious and deadly opposition from Luftwaffe interceptors. To counter this threat, the development of long-range fighters to escort the bombers had become one of the USAAF's highest priority projects.

The wartime problem was solved by the development of long-range escort fighters, but as the war was ending, the USAAF was beginning to develop bombers such as the Boeing B-50 and Convair B-36, whose range was three to five times greater than that of the bombers that had been used against Germany. This necessitated the development of escort fighters capable of matching the longer range, a problematic situation which led to the consideration of other, more radical, solutions.

As early as the summer of 1944, when the USAAF was pondering its dilemma, the idea of developing an escort fighter that could be *carried* by a bomber was proposed. Even then, it really wasn't a new idea. In the early 1930s Curtiss F9C-2 Sparrowhawk fighters had successfully conducted similar operations on a routine basis, flying from a 'trapeze' apparatus slung beneath the US Navy dirigibles *Akron* and *Macon*. The idea of conducting such operations from bombers flying at much higher speeds presented a great many additional problems. Not the least of these was the fact that the weight of the fighter would cut the bomb load proportionally. Future bombers, however, would be bigger, so if a fighter could be made smaller, a workable equation was theoretically possible.

Early in 1945, the USAAF's Air Technical Services Command (ATSC) began sounding out various airplane builders on the idea of building an ultra lightweight 'parasite' fighter that could be carried by the new, larger bombers that would be coming on-line in the late 1940s. McDonnell Aircraft of St Louis, a new, and certainly eager, company was willing to give it a try. McDonnell's original proposal was submitted in March 1945, and in October the USAAF ordered two prototypes under the designation XP-85, and with the stipulation that the resulting fighters had to fit entirely *within* a B-36 bomb bay.

In September 1947, the USAAF became the US Air Force, and in July 1948, the latter took delivery of the first XP-85 at Muroc (now Edwards) AFB, which was redesignated XF-85 under the Air Force policy of designating fighters as fighters rather than as pursuit planes.

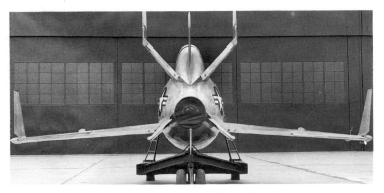

Above and right: The diminutive McDonnell XF-85 Goblin was a subject worth pondering. It was the world's *smallest* jet fighter.

The XF-85, which was named Goblin because of James Smith McDonnell's belief in the spirit world, was the smallest jet fighter that would ever be built. It was a tiny, rotund creature that looked more like an amusement park airplane than a serious Air Force program. The Goblin was only 15 feet long, with a wingspan of 21 feet. Its gross weight was 5600 pounds. It was powered by a Westinghouse J34 turbojet, and could be launched at altitudes up to 48,200 feet. Its performance could thus be maximized, because—unlike most fighters—it wouldn't have to expend time and fuel getting to altitude.

In the proposed scenario, B-36s deep inside enemy territory would, upon encountering enemy interceptors, release a swarm of Goblins to chase them away. The F-85s would have a duration of an hour or more, which was considered adequate for the job. The Goblin *would* fit into a B-36, and it looked good on paper, but somehow the idea of F-85s chasing MiG-17s is somewhat surreal.

The first 'parasite-ready' B-36 wasn't yet available, so the XF-85 test flights, that began on 28 August 1948, were conducted from a B-29 fitted with the 'trapeze' that was designed for the B-36. There were only seven flights conducted, but the XF-85 pilot was able to reattach the Goblin to the trapeze in only three of these. In the cases of these aborts, he had to bring the tiny airplane in for belly landings because it was designed without landing gear.

By 1949, it had become clear to the Air Force that parasite fighters would not be a practical solution to the escort fighter program, and on 24 October, the XF-85 program was terminated. Both prototypes were, however, preserved rather than being scrapped.

The Goblin lived and died in an era when the Air Force was keen to try anything. In any other time, it is doubtful that any funding—much less the $3 million that was actually spent on the XF-85—could be found for such a project. In the end it was a marginally viable idea that was complicated by an airplane whose silly appearance no one could take seriously.

Above and facing page, above: The XF-85 was first tested in August 1948 over the Mojave Desert. A B-29 carried it aloft and then extended the parasite on an elaborate 'trapeze.' The Goblin was then released to scamper home on its own. The XF-85 was designed to equip the giant B-36 bombers (*lower right*) but was never carried by any aircraft other than a single B-29 (*below*), which was the only aircraft ever equipped with an operational XF-85 trapeze.

The Curtiss XP-87 Blackhawk

Between 1920 and 1940, if one were to have asked 'who is the leading builder of US Army Air Corps fighters?' the answer would have been easy: the Glenn Curtiss Company, of course. The company founded by the man who had been to airplanes what Henry Ford had been to automobiles, ruled the field. From the early postwar biplanes, to the great P-40 Warhawk, Curtiss dominated the Air Corps' inventory of pursuit ships, and was a major player in the US Navy's arsenal as well.

During World War II, however, the scene began to change. By 1943, the P-40 had been eclipsed by aircraft such as the P-47, P-51 and F6F, and Curtiss had been eclipsed by such manufacturers as Lockheed, Republic and North American, who had played only minor roles before the war, but who were destined to remain on center stage in the postwar market.

Even before the end of World War II, all of these competitors were developing the jet fighters with which they intended to hold their places on that stage. Indeed, after 1944, the US Army Air Forces were simply not interested in any new fighter designs which were not jet-propelled.

Curtiss had its first opportunity to get into the USAAF jet fighter field as it responded to a November 1945 request by the USAAF for an all-weather jet fighter. The request had been formulated out of the experience of 11 months earlier during the Battle of the Bulge when the Germans launched a major offensive during a period of heavy clouds and snowfall, when Allied tactical airpower was grounded.

Curtiss proposed a variation of the now-cancelled XA-43 attack plane, and the USAAF responded favorably, ordering two fighter prototypes in December under the designation XP-87. Curtiss completed a mockup by July 1946, but USAAF records recall that the government was displeased. The instrument panel had 'numerous instruments and dials of the same size and

similar in function. Needless duplication was also apparent and the instrument panel seemed completely out of proportion. The [inspection] board was also dissatisfied with the bomb bay.'

Curtiss went back to work and the prototype XP-87 Black-hawk was finally ready for her first flight in March 1948. She was a cumbersome and unimaginative airplane, by comparison to the crisp simplicity of earlier Curtiss 'Hawks.' She was 65.5 feet long, with a wingspan of 60 feet, and had a design gross weight of 38,866 pounds—more than four times that of the P-40, which in turn had overall dimensions roughly half those of the XP-87. The powerplant consisted of four Westinghouse J34 turbojets, each delivering 3000 pounds of thrust.

Cursed from the beginning, the Blackhawk's first two 'crashes' took place before her first flight. These came in two traffic accidents suffered during November while she was being trucked from Columbus, Ohio to the test facilities at Muroc Army Air Field (now Edwards AFB).

Flight testing demonstrated the Blackhawk to be sluggish, with a poor rate of climb and a tendency toward hazardous buffeting at speeds over 300 mph. In short, the XP-87 was inferior to World War II piston-engined fighters. She was just too heavy for her engines' capacity to push her uphill, a factor that was due in part to the armor required by the USAAF (US Air Force after September 1947), and by the large quantities of heavy electronic gear required to achieve her all weather capability.

During flight tests she was compared to the Northrop XF-89 Scorpion, which outflew the poor XP-87 at every turn. The Scorpion was also a heavy straight-winged airplane, but it was clearly superior. Major General EM Powers, in evaluating the two planes, commented that the XP-87 'had proved to be a poor weapon from a performance standpoint and that it had many deficiencies aerodynamically.'

On 14 October 1948, the Blackhawk program was terminated. The unfinished second prototype was delivered for use as a 'spare parts stockpile' and in May 1949, the aircraft were stripped and cut up for scrap.

The last of the Curtiss 'Hawks'—and indeed the last Curtiss airplane—the ill-conceived Blackhawk had hastened the end of, and became the epilogue to, the Curtiss legend.

Below: The Curtiss XP-87 Blackhawk was sluggish and mediocre. It was the last fighter that Curtiss ever built and a pitiful end to a great lineage. The program was folded after the completion of only the single prototype *shown here*.

The Republic XF-84H

During World War II, Republic Aviation emerged as a major builder of fighter aircraft with its remarkable P-47 Thunderbolt. After the war, Republic, like all the other great wartime fighter-makers, turned its attention to jet fighters. The result was the P-84 (F-84 after 1947) Thunderjet, a straight-winged jet fighter which played an important role in the Korean War that was parallel to that played in World War II by the P-47. The Thunderjet evolved into the swept-winged F-84F (originally designated F-96) Thunderstreak, which first flew in 1952. The Thunderstreak, in turn, led to several other subvariants, including the RF-84F Thunderflash reconnaissance aircraft, and the XF-84H.

The idea behind the XF-84H was to take the basic F-84F *jet* and revamp it with a *turboprop* engine! It is hard to imagine what the US Air Force had in mind with this apparent retrogression, but two prototypes were ordered in December 1952. Not completed until nearly three years later, the first XF-84H had a wingspan of 33 feet 6 inches, an inch less than the F-84F, but was 55 feet 4 inches long—12 feet greater than the F-84F—because of the gargantuan propeller spinner attached to the huge Allison XT40-A-1 turboprop engine. The 29,700 pound gross weight of

the XF-84H was 20 percent higher than that of the F-84F, also because of the big experimental Allison engine. Unlike those of most propeller-driven aircraft, but like those of the P-39 and P-75 discussed earlier in this book, the engine was located behind the cockpit and linked to the propeller by a long driveshaft.

The first flight of the XF-84H, on 22 July 1955, confirmed the aircraft as being the *noisiest* single-engined aircraft ever produced, and noisier than many four-motored airplanes. This, however, was the only superlative ever attached to this bastardized Thunderstreak. Only 12 flights were made by the two XF-84H prototypes, yet all but one of these ended with *emergency landings*!

All of these flights—spanning nearly 15 months—were made by Republic test pilots, because the Air Force repeatedly *refused* to accept this dreadful airplane, even though it had bought 2711 F-84Fs. None of the harrowing test flights came near the advertised top speed of 670 mph, and the whole project was cancelled at last in October 1956.

The dreadful Republic XF-84H *(below)* was a development of the fine F-84F Thunderstreak *(right)*.

The Republic XF-91 Thunderceptor

It was another of that wonderful array of mutant creations born of the postwar era when the US Air Force would buy practically any proposal from any manufacturer—whatever strange tangent it was on—if the proposal promised to stretch the limits of performance.

Like that of the XF-84H, the airframe of the XF-91 was loosely based on that of Republic's F-84F Thunderstreak, the swept wing version of the F-84 which had been the company's first jet fighter, and like the XF-84H, the centerpiece of the XF-91 involved a foray into unorthodox engine technology.

The idea for swept wings had been derived from German engineering data captured at the end of World War II, and was being enthusiastically embraced by such American planemakers as Boeing, North American, and now Republic as well. Republic advanced their idea in October 1945, only a month after the end of World War II, although the airframe wasn't finalized for two years. The original idea involved throwing all the state of the art German—and American—research data into one pot and

stirring up the fastest possible interceptor. Among this technology was the notion of rocket propulsion, which had been barely operational on the German Me-163, but which was still largely untried and experimental as a means of powering *manned* aircraft.

Chuck Yeager broke the sound barrier in the rocket-powered Bell X-1 in 1947, but the X-1 in all its variations was strictly experimental (entirely dependent upon air-drop launches, rather than runway takeoffs) and never intended for production. The XF-91, on the other hand, was to be only one step short of the F-91, an operational supersonic interceptor.

The operational scenario was itself reminiscent of the German Me-163, insofar as the F-91 was intended for point defense. In other words, the aircraft would be based near potential targets and launched as enemy bombers closed in. In theory, the F-91 would take off and climb as high as 47,500 in less than 150 seconds, where it would have three minutes to kill the bombers with its four 20 mm cannons, and five minutes to get home before the rocket engines ran out of fuel.

The XF-91 was 43 feet 3 inches long, an inch shorter than the F-84F, with a wingspan of 31 feet 3 inches, two feet less than its predecessor. The wings themselves had a highly distinctive inverse taper, a characteristic that was designed by Republic's Alexander Kartveli to provide greater lift, while permitting high-speed flight and lower-speed (and thus shorter) landings and take-offs without stalling. Republic intended that the production F-91s have 'V-shaped' tails, but installed traditional tail surfaces, like those intended for the F-84F, in the two prototypes.

Power was to be supplied by four Curtiss-Wright XLR27 rocket engines delivering a total of 4000 pounds of thrust, but this proposed power plant was cancelled in favor of a Reaction Motors (later Morton Thiokol) XLR11 engine delivering 6000 pounds of thrust. The rocket power was to be supplemented by a General Electric J47 afterburning turbojet engine, delivering 5000 pounds of thrust.

The power inherent in the XF-91 Thunderceptor was nothing short of awesome, but as early as August 1947, the US Army Air Forces (US Air Force as of one month later) Aircraft & Weapons Board shelved the idea of using the big airplane as an interceptor.

Thus it was that the XF-91—which was completed three years ahead of its brother F-84F—came into the world as a research airplane rather than as a potential combat aircraft. The name 'Thunderceptor' was now a misnomer, but it nonetheless remained, perhaps with a hope on Republic's part that the intended role would be revived. The first of only two Thunderceptors was finished in March 1949 and shipped from Republic's Farmingdale, New York plant to the Air Force test center at Edwards AFB, where it arrived *two years* ahead of the XLR11 rocket engine.

Using only the turbojet, flight tests began on 9 May 1949 with Republic's Carl Bellinger at the controls. The afterburner, however, was not tested for six months. The second XF-91 first flew in June 1951, having been the first of the two to be equipped with the XLR11.

Pilots disliked the XF-91, just as they disliked rocket engines.

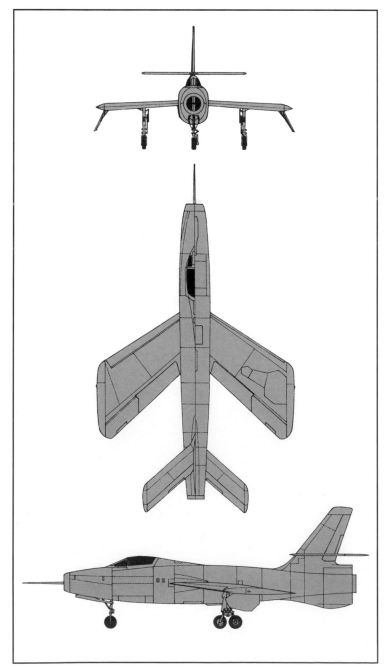

The large intake of the first XF-91 (*left and top right*) evolved into a scoop-type on the second aircraft (*right*). Note the rocket engine under the tail.

They were incredibly unpredictable and downright dangerous, and the test pilots all knew the litany of stories about the large numbers of unmanned rockets that just blew up. The XLR11 itself had blown up on a test stand in January 1951, and the second XF-91 had suffered an engine fire in its turbojet on its third flight the following June. It was not a very auspicious beginning for the Thunderceptor program, which was two years old without the rocket motor having yet been tested in flight.

The first flight test of the XLR11 was in fact unplanned, and added more fuel to the XF-91's bad reputation. On 11 September 1952, the J47 turbojet flamed out during takeoff, and the pilot had to fire the rocket to kick the plane high enough in order to come around for an emergency landing.

The first planned airborne firing of the XLR11, one week later on 18 September, was a major disappointment in that the XF-91 was unable to accelerate to its intended top speed. The aircraft was designed for Mach 1.4, but at Mach 1.18, it began to shimmy and shake so badly that Republic test pilot Russell 'Rusty' Roth didn't dare push it any higher. This was profoundly bad news, considering that it came more than three years after flight testing had begun.

Two days later the rocket engine exploded, nearly blowing the tail off the aircraft. Though the program continued, both Republic and the Air Force had lost interest. Wanting to devote its resources to the F-84F program, Republic officially asked the Air Force on 29 April 1954 that the project be terminated. Strangely, it took the Air Force five months to concur with the request.

The Thunderceptor program cost the American taxpayer $11.7 million, and took five years and 192 flights to prove what any Me-163 pilot could have confirmed in 1945, and that is that rocket-powered interceptors were—and still are—unreliable and impractical.

Below and right: Two views of the second XF-91 after its retirement to the Air Force Museum at Wright-Patterson AFB.

Flying Cars and 'Roadable' Airplanes

The concept of vehicles that could transform themselves from automobiles to airplanes dates back to the earliest days that the two both existed. The ubiquitous Glenn Curtiss produced a design for a three-seat flying car in time for the Pan-American Aeronautic Exposition in New York in February 1917. It flew, but poorly, and was scrapped. Subsequent literature ranges from stories of backyard tinkerers to the fantasies that Ian Fleming imagined to get James Bond out of tight situations. There was, of course, Waldo Waterman's Studebaker-engined Arrowbile in 1937 and the Pitcairn PA-36 Whirlwing of 1939, a mongrel autogiro that was actually designed by Juan de la Cierva.

Despite the alluring appeal of these vehicles, they are an instance where theory and practicality never crossed paths. In the optimistic days after World War II, however, anything seemed possible. Technology promised backyard heliports and suggested that ownership of private airplanes would be as common in the late 1940s as automobile ownership had been in the 1930s. It was only reasonable, therefore, to predict a solid market for flying cars. Dozens were proposed, and some were actually built and flight tested.

The Boggs Airmaster, designed by HD Boggs and marketed by Buzz Hershfeld, included a 16 foot car with a 35 foot wingspan powered by a 145 hp engine, but it was never built. The Spratt Controllable Wing car, which appeared in late 1945, featured a pusher prop and a flexible wing mounted on a swivel behind the two-passenger cab. George Spratt later teamed up with William B Stout (who had merged his Stout Aircraft Company into Consolidated Vultee), in a vain effort to market the vehicle under the tradename Skycar.

The unique Hervey Travelplane, which also appeared in 1947, had a single dural tail boom which passed *through* the pusher propeller shaft to support the tail surfaces. The propeller was, in turn, driven by a 200 hp Ranger engine that promised four hours of air time at 125 mph. Designed by George Hervey of Roscoe, California, the Travelplane had a 16 foot automobile and a 36 foot wingspan. Conversion from airplane to automobile took six minutes when Hervey demonstrated it, although customers might spend a bit more time — an hour or so — until they learned the ropes. The wings could then be stored in a 'convenient' trailer unit. There was no provision, however, for airlifting the trailer.

The Whitaker-Zuck Planemobile was 19 feet long, with 32.5 feet of folding wings. Built in 1947, it solved the problem of what to do with the wings by simply folding them across its back, to

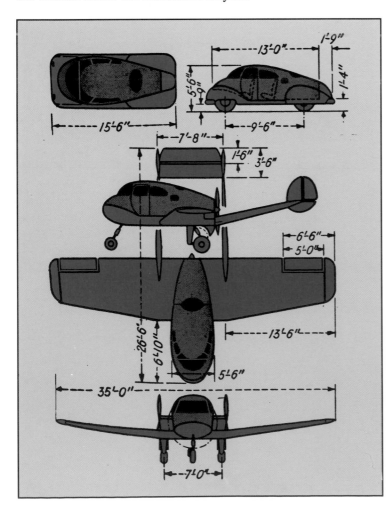

Ted Hall's original idea in mating an automobile to an airplane was to develop a design that paratroops and commandos could use.

Drive Right Up

A FLYING automobile with a 130-hp. Franklin engine cruises at 110 m.p.h. in the air and travels 60 m.p.h. on the road. Those speeds were set by the first model of a design by Ted Hall, aviation engineer. Portable Products Corp., Garland, Tex., is considering the possibilities of producing it.

The "roadable" plane has detachable propeller, wing, booms, and tail. The forward end of the engine crankshaft turns the prop, while a shaft extends aft from the engine into a conventional automobile transmission and differential. Power goes both to propeller and rear wheels for the take-off.

With its 30-foot wing and its tail removed, the flying auto looks pretty much like other cars on a highway. Its chassis is conventional.

Hall's three-wheel, "roadable" airplane seats only two, but has ample luggage space in the rear. Rear wheels are on shock struts.

be carried like a hermit crab carries his shell. The Taylor Aerocar, built by Molton Taylor of Longview, Washington in 1949, was a V-tailed bird whose wings folded neatly into a self-contained trailer for easy towing.

Robert E Fulton's FA-3 Airphibian was not amphibious but rather 'airphibious,' a two-place airplane whose forward fuselage could simply 'drive away' from the rest of the airplane upon landing. It first flew on 7 November 1946, but never progressed beyond the prototype stage.

Of all the projects that developed in those idealistic days after the war, there were none that came so close to getting into the commercial mainstream than the creations of Theodore P 'Ted' Hall, an engineer at Consolidated Vultee Aircraft in San Diego, who quit his job at the end of the war to pursue his dream. Joined by Tommy Thompson, a friend and former Consolidated colleague, Hall began work on his dream in 1945. Forming the light-gauge aluminum sheets with a rubber hammer around a tube steel framework, Hall, Thompson and their small crew set about to hand make the first prototype. They picked a 90 hp Franklin to power the airplane part, and lifted a four-cylinder

Flying auto is this strange vehicle, perfected by famous flyer Waldo Waterman. A car on the highways, it adds wings at its hangar and smoothly takes to the skyways. Its power plant is a 6-cylinder Studebaker Dictator engine which operates on ordinary filling station gas.

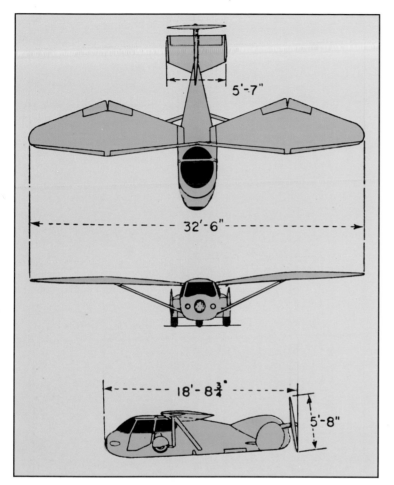

These pages, from left: The Boggs Airmaster Air Car, Ted Hall's Flying Car, the Whitaker-Zuck Plane-Mobile and *(above)* Waldo Waterman's Arrowbile is tagged for speeding in a 1937 Studebaker advertisement. Waterman used Studebaker engines.

26.5 hp engine from an old Crosley auto for the car half. In fact their compact little vehicle, whose interior was about the same size as a Volkswagen 'Beetle,' looked a bit like a Crosley, except for its being mounted on a three-wheel chassis.

Having completed the Hall Flying Car, the southern California entrepreneurs successfully test flew it, and wound up being the subject of a feature in a 1946 issue of *Popular Science* magazine. In the meantime, Hall and Thompson had been beating the bushes for someone who would underwrite the production of their brainchild. A proposed deal with Portable Products Corporation in Garland, Texas had gone by the wayside, when Hall struck a deal with his former employer.

Suffering a severe sag in airplane orders because of the end of the war, Consolidated Vultee Aircraft (now known as Convair) was keen for new business, and the conventional wisdom was that the United States was on the threshold of an unprecedented boom in general aviation. Every major airplane manufacturer was anxious to cash in on the 'airplane in every garage' future, and Convair was no different, so they bought out Ted Hall and moved the project into their main plant at Lindbergh Field near San Diego. Convair predicted a huge market for Hall's vehicle among travelling salesmen. They even went so far as to buy the

Stinson Aircraft Company—a well-known general aviation manufacturer—as a conduit for producing and marketing it. They also had acquired Stout Aircraft, which was, as noted above, also involved in a similar project.

A second version of the Flying Car was developed, which differed from the original by its having a conventional four-wheel layout on the car, and a single, rather than double, rudder arrangement. This craft, now designated as the Convair Model 118 ConvAirCar, was ready to fly in July 1946. Hall and a Convair test pilot took it up to 2000 feet, made a couple of turns over the field and touched down. Convair management was delighted. They predicted minimum sales of 160,000 units with a retail price tag of $1500. The wings would be extra, but you could pick those up at any airport on a one-way rental basis.

Ultimately, however, only two Model 118s were built, with the second being completed in 1947. This ConvAirCar incorporated the fiberglass body envisioned for the production models, and had a 190 hp Pratt & Whitney radial engine that could propel the vehicle at 125 mph in the air.

Early in November 1947, misfortune struck. The second ConvAirCar took off on a routine flight during which the pilot misjudged his fuel. They ran out of gas and were forced to make an emergency landing on a dirt road. The pilot walked away, but the wings sheared off and the fiberglass body was beyond repair.

In a decision based on the publicity surrounding the crash, and the huge number of cheap former-military airplanes flooding the market, Convair abandoned the program and sold the hardware back to Ted Hall. He is reported to have retired to New York, although the prototype ConvAirCars are reported to be in a warehouse in El Cajon, California.

The end of the ConvAirCar was really the end of practical hope for flying cars in the United States. If a company like Convair, with all its resources, couldn't do it, then it probably wasn't going to be economically viable. In retrospect, there is a certain allure held by flying cars on a warm summer evening in Southern California, but when one pictures 160,000—or even 160—flying cars airborne during a January storm over Chicago, New York or London, the idea is a lot less practical. In the very areas where the people live who would make use of flying cars, the airspace is much too crowded for such flimsy craft flown by pilots with marginal experience.

Below: The single-tailed Convair Model 118 ConvAirCar of 1947 had evolved out of Ted Hall's twin-tailed Flying Car. Convair, who built some of the most important conventional aircraft of the day, had high hopes for the ConvAirCar, but only two Model 118s had been completed by November 1947, when an empty gas tank precipitated a crash landing. Neither person in the car was killed, but the program was a fatality. It was not the last flying automobile, but it was the last to be taken seriously by a major planemaker. *Bottom:* The Hervey Model 25 Travelplane was planned as a midwing-pusher, four-place roadable to be powered by a 200-hp Ranger. The top speed was estimated at 135 mph, with a range of four hours at 125-mph cruising speed. A two-control spinproof, stallproof system was to have been incorporated, in addition to scoop-type ailerons like those on the World War II-era Northrop P-61 Black Widow fighter aircraft.

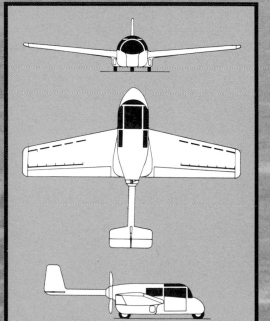

The Saunders-Roe Princess

The Princess was Britain's answer to Howard Hughes' *Spruce Goose*, one part grandiose vision for each part pure folly. She was, like the Hughes-Kaiser HK-1, a product of the dream of conquering the world's oceans by flying over them. In post-war Britain, commercial navigation of the world's airways was seen as being as essential to maintaining the empire as Britain's maritime domination of the globe had been in the nineteenth century. Thus it was that the Princess was really more a political venture than an economically justifiable commercial one.

The company that was chosen to build these grand flying boats seemed sturdy enough, being a partnership of Sammy Saunders of Goring-on-Thames, purveyor of great speedboats to the great and near-great, and AV Roe, purveyor of great airplanes to the Royal Air Force. Yet their collaborations had included only the unsuccessful wartime Lerwick flying boat, and the equally abortive SRA-1 seaplane jet fighter.

More than a flying boat, the Saunders-Roe Princess was a flying ocean liner. Aside from the Hughes-Kaiser Hk-1, she was the biggest amphibian ever attempted, with a length of 148 feet and a wingspan of 219.5 feet. Her gross weight was 345,000 pounds and she could cruise at 350 mph for 6000 miles. Her projected passenger capacity of 220 would not be matched by another commercial airliner until the advent of the Boeing 747 a quarter century later. She was a source of pride to the Labour Government that led Britain out of the war years, although BOAC, the national airline that would actually have to use the Princess, was dubious. Nevertheless, the government insisted on pressing ahead with not just one prototype, but three.

Like any great technological leap with a timetable set by politicians, the Princess took longer than expected to evolve. Work began in 1946 with a projected completion date of 1948. By 1949, however, the first Princess prototype was still under construction and waiting for suitable engines, while Britain's Labour Government was assuring BOAC that the plane would fly in 1950.

Finally, the big, 2500 hp Bristol Proteus turboprops were made available and the Princess was equipped with ten. Eight were doubled up in the four inboard nacelles to drive four sets of contra-rotating propellers, and two were installed conventionally. These latter two were to be the only parts of the whole system that didn't provide a chronic nightmare for maintenance.

By the time the first Princess (call letters G-ALUN) was ready to go in 1952, the Conservative party was in power in Britain, and they were furious that the previous Labour Government had spent nearly four times the originally estimated £3 million on the trio of monster seaplanes. Also, by the early 1950s,

conventional wisdom within the world's airline industry had rejected seaplanes in favor of land planes as the standard for future high density air routes. The result was that the second two Princesses were never completed, and the first was relegated to serving only as a demonstrator, a flying novelty, something akin to a proud racehorse being relegated to giving pony rides to little children.

Saunders and Roe themselves continued to play with the fantasy of even larger flying boats, such as the huge, thousand-passenger P-192 that would have had a 313-foot wingspan, and have been powered by two dozen jet engines. The Princesses, however, died a sad death, being unceremoniously cut up for scrap in 1967, by which time the whole idea of grand flying boat liners was just an archaic bit of history, a quaint notion from a bygone age.

Below and overleaf: The G-ALUN was the only one of the series of three Princesses planned by Saunders-Roe to actually be completed.

The Bristol Brabazon

The Princesses were not the only larger than life vision of the future of commercial aviation to arise in Britain after the war. There was also the pretentious Bristol Model 167 Brabazon, a huge land plane that took its name from Aircraft Production Minister Lord Brabazon, who proposed the concept in 1943. Here again, as with the Princess, the idea was politically rather than commercially motivated, an element in the effort to keep the Empire together through technological virtuosity.

As it is with political projects, money is never an object—until the project has turned from a sparkling, visionary concept to a gritty machine running behind schedule. This was a case of a single airplane that cost British taxpayers £12.5 million, and wound up being sold for £10,000 in scrap value. As it was with Brabazon, the war had ended before it was much more than a pile of very large blueprints spread across the hangar floor. The

first flight, postponed to 1947, took place on 4 September 1949.

The Brabazon prototype (call letters G-AGPW) was a remarkable airplane if only for its size. It was the largest airplane to ever take off from a runway, being 15 feet longer, at 177 feet, than the Americans' big Convair B-36 bomber. (The two planes had identical wingspans of 230 feet, and roughly equal gross weights in the 100-ton range.) Both of these planes were wonders of postwar technology of the school that held for basically scaling up wartime designs by a factor of two or more. It was a notion that wreaked of obsolescence lurking just under the surface, but such a prophecy was hardly evident as you beheld such a gleaming colossus.

For the Brabazon, however, lurking obsolescence took many forms. First of all, she was late. The B-36 had been flying for three years, but on the commercial side, the air routes were filled

with the likes of Boeing Stratocruisers and bigger and better Lockheed Constellations, not to mention the faint smell of jet fuel just beyond the horizon. Then there were the engines. Bristol had installed eight of its own Centaurus radial engines driving contra-rotating propellers, but they left the poor Brabazon grossly underpowered.

The proposed solution was to replace the Centaurus piston engines with Proteus turboprops, but the latter were, even at that same moment, causing a hat full of headaches for the engineers at Saunders-Roe who were trying to use them in the Princess flying boat. It seems that when geared to contra-rotating propellers, the Proteus was nothing but trouble, and the Brabazon simply couldn't make do with four engines of any kind, and having been designed with only four nacelles, the only way to go was with two engines in each, driving contra-rotating props.

It is easy to blame bad timing and/or bad engines for the failure of any airplane, but the Brabazon with fraught with more than its own share of design flaws. Her wings were big and heavy. They were designed that way so as to submerge the engines within them aerodynamically, but the byproduct of the design was that in any but the best weather conditions, they had the potential to scrape on the runway during landing. They were also so stiff that the Ministry of Transport wouldn't grant the Brabazon an airworthiness certificate to operate above 25,000 feet, an environment that is essential for practical airliner traffic. Finally, there were problems with metal fatigue, which was far worse that lurking obsolescence, it was lurking catastrophe!

By the end of 1952, the creaking leviathan was a white elephant in the clearest sense of the word. She couldn't do what she was supposed to do, and nobody wanted her. Technically, she *could* have done as intended, that is to fly 100 passengers nonstop from London to New York or Cairo, but within a few years, jetliners were hauling half again more people in half the time it would have taken the Brabazon to do the job.

In July 1953, the single completed Brabazon and a half-finished sister were declared surplus and cut up for scrap. Only a single gargantuan nose wheel survives as a reminder of Britain's largest airliner.

Below: Along with the Saunders-Roe Princess of the previous pages, the Bristol Brabazon was intended to herald a new era in British commercial aviation. Like the Princess, however, only one Brabazon was ever flown. It was a huge and underpowered aircraft that consumed a great deal of time and money before it was finally and mercifully scrapped.

The Avro Tudor

As World War II was winding down, a great many people in aviation circles began to look toward postwar civilian applications for the big, long-range warplanes that had been developed *during* the war. As had been the case after World War I, the aircraft makers who had built the big bombers were among those who longed the hardest for such applications.

Britain's AV Roe & Company, Ltd (Avro) had produced the Empire's most successful family of four-engined bombers— which included the Lancaster and Lincoln—and they had begun thinking of commercial applications as early as 1942. Indeed,

Avro's Model 685 York, which first flew in July of that year, was an airliner whose wings and tail were virtually identical to those of the Lancaster, and it entered service with British Overseas (BOAC) in 1944. The Avro Model 691 Lancastrian, which was even more like the Lancaster, entered service with BOAC in May 1945, giving AV Roe the distinction of having *two* bomber-derived airliner types on commercial routes before the war ended.

Having done this, the next step was to develop an airliner that was a whole generation ahead of the Lancaster. This was to be

the Avro Model 688 and 689 Tudor. The new design was based more on the Lincoln than on the Lancaster, with a strong resemblance to the American Douglas DC-4, a four-engined airliner which had appeared immediately prior to the war.

The Tudor was to be 85 feet long with a wingspan of 120 feet and a gross weight of 80,000 pounds. This made it almost exactly the same size as the DC-4 and the Lockheed Constellation, although the latter's gross weight was about a quarter again greater. The Tudor promised a range of up to 4000 miles, twice that of the other planes, although they had passenger capacities that were double that of the Tudor's 32.

Things looked great for the Tudor, with 99 aircraft presold to BOAC, Qantas and South African Airways by April 1945. However, when the first one flew two months later, things began to turn sour. The Tudor was difficult to fly and suffered greatly from the decision to not adopt a tricycle landing gear, which the Yanks were already using on the DC-4, the Constellation and the Douglas DC-6. BOAC didn't care for the Tudor and found so many things that they wanted changed that they wound up by cancelling their order. Only 22 were built and most of these wound up with British South American Airways (BSAA).

The smaller Tudor 2, which was introduced in 1946, showed no improvement in its handling characteristics. BOAC reluctantly ordered 18, and six more went to BSAA, where the Tudor ended its career hauling freight over the Andes.

Below: An Avro Tudor C, Mk 1, powered by Merlin 600 engines as seen in BOAC colors in October 1946. BOAC ridded itself of Tudors ASAP.

The Lockheed XFV-1 and The Convair XFY-1 Pogo

The idea of vertical take-off and landing (VTOL) for high-performance fighters has been a perplexing and obsessive one for aircraft designers for years. Helicopters and autogiros could take off vertically, but they were—until the 1980s—perceived as being too fragile, too slow and too vulnerable for the world of intense aerial combat. The British Aerospace Harrier, which evolved in the late 1960s, and proved itself so well in the Falklands War in 1982, has been the only successful VTOL fighter yet developed, but it has not been for want of trying. The original idea (which was eventually discarded in the case of the Harrier) was fairly simple. It involved standing the airplane on its tail, giving it a powerful engine and taking off straight up.

The first serious attempts at developing a VTOL fighter were probably those undertaken in Germany during World War II at a time when Allied bombers were destroying German airfields, and thus creating a need for VTOL aircraft. The Bachem Natter may be considered a precursor, but it was really designed for vertical take-off alone. Landing was not considered to be a necessary part of the scenario. While the Natter was being developed, work was proceeding on the idea of a recoverable and reusable VTOL fighter. These efforts originated with Heinz von Halem at the Focke-Wulf Aircraft Company in September 1944.

The aircraft that von Halem proposed was called Triebfluegel. It was a wingless airplane with a huge, three-bladed propeller around its waist. This propeller, whose diameter was greater than the length of the fuselage itself, was powered by a vectorable ramjet engine at the tip of each blade. The Focke-Wulf Triebfluegel would need no runway. It could take off from any patch of level ground. Had there been enough time left in the war for the Triebfluegel to actually go into production, it might have been the ideal air defense fighter, because the Luftwaffe could have based it almost anywhere.

After World War II, the US Navy became interested in the same idea. It would be to their advantage to have a fighter aircraft to provide air defense for operations that might take place when and where an aircraft carrier would not be available. In March 1951, less than a year after the start of the Korean War, the Navy ordered prototype VTOL fighters from both Lockheed and Convair under the designations XFV-1 and XFY-1. Both would be designed around the huge, 6825 hp Allison XT40-A-16 double turboprop engine, and whichever design proved itself superior, would be ordered into production.

The first Lockheed XFV-1 was completed in 1953. It stood 36 feet 10 inches in its vertical stance, had straight wings that spanned 30 feet 11 inches, and had a gross weight of 16,221 pounds. However, the XT40-A-16 wasn't ready, so the XFV-1

Opposite page: A team from Lockheed gamely regards the only prototype XFV-1 at Muroc Army Air Field. *Below:* The Lockheed XFV-1—with and without the elaborate crew access gantry.

was fitted with the less-powerful 5332 hp XT40-A-14. Because of this, it was decided not to attempt any vertical takeoffs, and the aircraft was fitted with a crude auxiliary landing gear for horizontal take-offs. Taxi tests began in December 1953, and test pilot Herman 'Fish' Salmon made the first horizontal take-off on 16 June 1954. In the course of 32 test flights, Salmon never made a vertical take-off, but while in flight, he made the transition from horizontal to vertical mode many times.

Convair's delta-winged XFY-1 stood 32 feet 3 inches tall and had a wing span of 27 feet 8 inches. It was first flown by TF Coleman on 1 August 1954, six weeks after the XFV-1. Because the XFY-1 had a gross weight of 14,250 pounds, a ton lighter than the XFV-1, Convair decided to attempt a vertical takeoff. This proved successful, but both Convair and Lockheed would soon discover that it wasn't the takeoffs that were the inherent design flaw in the concept, it was the landings.

Because the pilot literally had to look over his shoulder to back one of these aircraft down, landings were considered

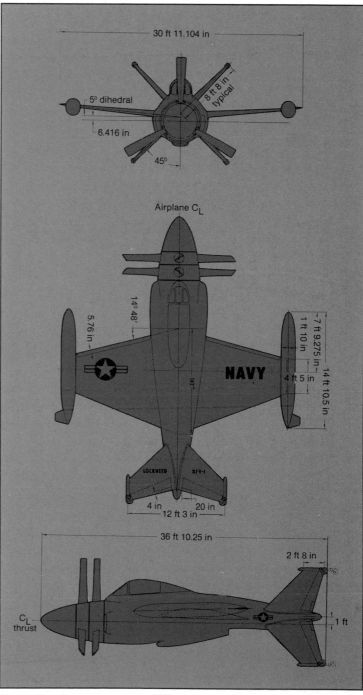

Above: The strange lines of the XFV-1 whose servicing rack (*left*) had better landing gear than the airplane itself.

impractical and even dangerous! Landing the airplanes on a sunny day at a test field was one matter, but imagine trying to land one on the pitching deck of a ship during bad weather or an enemy attack.

Kelly Johnson, the great aircraft designer who was responsible for many of Lockheed's greatest aircraft, never liked the concept. Said Johnson, 'We practiced landing on clouds, and we practiced looking over our shoulders. We couldn't tell how fast we were coming down, or when we would hit. We wrote the Navy: "We think it is inadvisable to *land* the airplane." They came back with one paragraph that said "We agree." '

Both the XFV-1 and XFY-1 programs were cancelled in 1955 at the request of the contractors. It was a decidedly unusual turn of events, but clearly neither firm wanted to be involved in the continuation of a project that was so clearly misguided. In the annals of bad aircraft there are many stories of airplanes which could not take off, but nowhere is there another story of two projects, so serious and well-funded, that produced aircraft which couldn't land.

Above: Unable to takeoff vertically, the XFV-1 was retrofitted for a horizontal takeoff. *Below and opposite:* It is easy to picture a pilot taking off in a Convair XFY-1, but hard to imagine how he could feel good about landing.

Below: Herman 'Fish' Salmon adjusts his oxygen mask as he glances back at the pilot of a chase plane pursuing him across the dry Mojave lakebeds where most American military aircraft testing has taken place since 1945. The peaks of the southern Sierra Nevada can be seen in the background. The XFV-1 was never provided with its promised 6825 hp Allison XT40-A-16 double turboprop and had to settle for a 5332 hp XT40-A-14, a compromise that prohibited the Lockheed XFV-1 from being able to takeoff vertically. As a result it was retrofitted with rickety, embarrassing, nonretractable landing gear for all of its test flights.

The Convair XF2Y-1 Sea Dart

The washout of the XFY-1 notwithstanding, Convair was pictured in the early 1950s as being *the* American plane-maker on the leading edge of technological innovation. There were so many feathers in Convair's cap that the cap rivalled the richly feathered headdress of a Cheyenne war chief. There was the B-36, now obsolescent, but still the world's biggest bomber. There was the XF-92, the world's first fighter with a true delta wing, which begat the operational F-102 Delta Dagger, which in turn led to the F-106 Delta Dart, which was being touted as the 'ultimate interceptor.' Convair also had on its horizon the spectacular B-58, which was a Mach 2 delta that was destined to be the world's first supersonic bomber. When it came to radical innovation and advancing technology, the dateline was Convair. These were heady days indeed.

It was against this backdrop that Convair's hydrodynamic research laboratory pushed the limits of innovation just a wee bit far by proposing to put an F-102 on *water skis*!

Convair hadn't had a seaplane in production since World War II, and there was an element of support within the company for perpetuating that tradition, even in the face of rapidly evolving aviation technology. Thus it was that the XF2Y program began to take shape in 1951. It was the kind of project that really flew in the face of practicality as well as going against the tide of aircraft evolution. Seaplanes, especially high performance seaplanes, were generically obsolescent in the 1950s and the US Navy knew it. There never would have been an XF2Y if it hadn't been that the Navy's aviation people had been in the throes of an inferiority crisis ever since the US Air Force was created in 1947. When it came to leading edge technology, the Navy strived to be second to no one. If the Air Force would have the Delta Dart, the Navy would have the Sea Dart!

First ordered in January 1951, the Sea Dart design was complete in mock up form by August 1952, when the order was increased from two to 12 aircraft. The Sea Dart had an overall

Below: The test pilot glances down during a 1953 taxi test in the original XF2Y-1.
Right: Looking here very futuristic against a surreal hand-tinted sunset, the XF2Y-1's dorsal intakes gave it unintended stealth characteristics.

shape and configuration that was very similar to that of the Air Force's F-102. The XF2Y-1 was 52 feet 7 inches long, an inch longer than the prototype YF-102. It had a wingspan of 33 feet 8 inches, compared to 37 feet for the YF-102. The Sea Dart had a gross weight of 21,500 pounds (18 percent less than the Air Force craft) and was powered by a Westinghouse J46 turbojet delivering 5725 pounds of thrust.

Much to the Navy's joy, the Sea Dart was even the first of the two to fly. With its maiden voyage of 9 April 1953 with ED Shannon at the controls, the XF2Y-1 beat the YF-102 by six months. Timing may have been cause for celebration at the Navy's Bureau of Aeronautics, but performance was not. The first Sea Dart suffered from vibration and instability after take-off because of the cumbersome twin-ski landing gear. The second prototype was completed with a single ski, but the program was, by now, in trouble. There was clearly no operational justification for high performance jet fighters to also be

seaplanes, and in March 1954 the F2Y production order, which now stood at 22 units, was cut back to just five.

The second prototype broke the sound barrier in a shallow dive on 3 August 1954, to become the first supersonic seaplane in history. However, this aircraft was lost in November 1954, four months before the third prototype made its initial flight. The fourth and fifth aircraft were completed but never flown. The program was terminated, having demonstrated a certain virtuosity, but without ever having demonstrated an operational rationale. The 1950s were an era in aviation which, in retrospect, held money as no object when technology was involved—it was an era when anything that *could* be tried, *was* tried, even if there was no observable reason. The Sea Dart was just another relic of that soon-to-be bygone epoch.

Facing page: The first XF2Y-1 in flight and setting down. *Below:* A sad old sea horse, circa 1969, put out to pasture.

The Myasishchyev Mya-4

The history of Soviet aviation has been one of intermittent true innovation obscured by all-too-frequent bureaucratic meddling and an obsessive inferiority complex that has led to knee-jerk copies of Western aircraft. From the Tupolev Tu-4 of 1946, which was a slavish copy of the Boeing B-29, to the Kosmolyet *Buran* of 1988, which was an almost verbatim attempt to duplicate the American Rockwell International Space Shuttle Orbiter, Soviet aerospace engineers have unashamedly knocked off the best the West has had to offer. Occasionally, however, there were the likes of the Mikoyan Gurovich MiG 15 of 1949, or the Antonov An-225 of 1988, that surprised the Western world by being truly ingenious designs. The Mya-4, and indeed the whole history of the Myasishchyev design bureau, were the antithesis of this notion.

As a young engineer, Vladimir Myasishchyev had worked at Tupolev on the Ant-20 (*Maksim Gorkii*) project, an assignment which no doubt whetted his taste for the grandiose. In 1937, as relations between the United States and the Soviet Union warmed in the sun of New Deal liberalism, he was part of a Soviet contingent invited to America to study the Yank aircraft industry. Vladimir was sent to Santa Monica, California to help copy the blueprints for the great Douglas DC-3 as part of the deal wherein the Lisunov design bureau would get to build the DC-3 under license. Ultimately they built thousands under the Li-2 designation without more than a passing thought to paying Douglas either a compliment or a royalty. This assignment probably equipped Vladimir with the notion that imitation, while perhaps the sincerest form of flattery, is certainly a short-cut to a good airplane.

After a brief run-in with the commissars back in the USSR over political incorrectness, Myasishchyev was rehabilitated in 1943 in time to head Petlyakov design bureau projects for the last years of World War II. He retired after the war, but was called back in 1949 for a special project. The cold war was at its depths and the Americans had a monopoly on atomic weapons (the Soviets would explode their first later in the year), and a commanding lead in long-range strategic bombers. The Soviets did not at that time possess the technology to build a jet-propelled bomber that could reach any of the United States save Alaska. Myasishchyev got the job.

The Tupolev design bureau was already at work on their Tu-20 'Bear' four-engined turboprop, which the Red air force saw as a hedge against Myasishchyev's possible failure.

Myasishchyev went to work, borrowing what he could from the Boeing B-47, and from what was then known about the Boeing B-52. The result was the Mya-4, an airplane that was to be known to fear mongers in the West as 'the Russian B-52'. It had centerline 'bicycle' landing gear like the B-47 and B-52, and was a huge, swept-wing beast. First flown in 1953, two years after the B-52, the Mya-4 was 155 feet long (later models were 20 feet longer), with a wingspan of up to 172 feet, making it almost the same size as the B-52. Its maximum gross weight of 460,000 pounds was roughly equal to the last models of the B-52.

In terms of power and performance, however, the Mya-4 never compared to the B-52, and never lived up to expectations. About 200 entered service after 1956, but as a type, the Mya-4 left a great deal to be desired. The four Mikulin AM3 turbojets buried in her wing roots delivered a total of 76,720 pounds of thrust, compared to more than half again more for the B-52's

Above left: A 1975 artist's conception of a twin-tailed Mya-4 being used to carry the Soviet Kosmolyet Space Shuttle Orbiter. It has since been replaced by the An-225. *Below and above right:* Mya-4 Bison B bombers with nose probe

refuelling booms. *Right:* The Bison C, the final Mya-4 bomber type, had an AS-2 Puff Ball radar probe in its nose and still retained external dorsal gun turrets, a feature rarely seen on American jet bombers of the period.

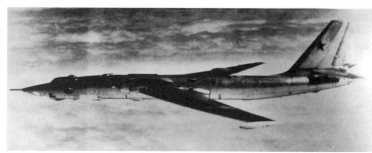

Pratt & Whitneys. Her normal range was about 6500 miles, which was really not enough to penetrate the heart of the United States, and was a good deal less than that of the B-52, or indeed that of Tupolev's Tu-20. Ironically, prop-driven Tu-20 bombers were still flying long-range missions to Cuba in the late 1980s, two decades after the Mya-4 was retired as a bomber.

They gave the Mya-4 the name Molot, which means hammer (NATO gave her the code name Bison), but she was a rubber hammer, a showpiece. Never taken seriously as a strategic bomber within the Soviet Air Force's Dalnaya Aviatsya (Strategic Air Command), the Molot fleet was retrofitted in the 1960s as aerial refuelling aircraft. In the early 1980s, at least one of the remaining Mya-4s was modified to carry the Soviet Kosmolyet Space Shuttle Orbiter on its early glide tests. This use was phased out in 1988 in favor of the newer and larger An-225 transport.

The Mya-4 was successful not as a strategic bomber, but as a weapon in the psychological trenches of the cold war, she did her job. In a sense, she was like a wooden gun. She looked real, but wouldn't have been able to deliver the blow. In the end, however, just looking the part was enough to do the job, to frighten the enemy. The Mya-4's most successful mission was flown on 1 May 1954, when she overflew the Moscow May Day parade in full view of Western spectators. They saw her size, but not her sluggish performance, and the hulking horror of the 'Russian B-52' haunted Western—notably US Air Force—planners for the next decade.

The Tupolev Tu-144

The dramatic advances in worldwide aviation technology between 1945 and 1960 were unparalleled, and, indeed, were predicted to continue. In those few short years jet aircraft had been introduced and the technology had evolved to the point where jetliners were not only practical, but they were in routine use. The sound barrier was broken in 1947, and within a decade there were dozens of aircraft worldwide that were capable of *double* the speed of sound. Against this backdrop, it was natural to assume that the era of the supersonic airliners was just around the corner. It was not a question of whether the future would include massive routine use of supersonic transports (SSTs), it was only a question of who would get first crack at the vast number of orders that would soon come rolling in.

Britain, France, the United States and the Soviet Union all entered the sweepstakes. The research and development effort in each country was as expensive as it was extensive. Even in the

United States, the SST project became so costly, yet had such a high priority, that the government helped to underwrite the endeavor.

In 1962, under the growing weight of financial pressure, the French and British governments agreed to merge their respective national efforts and work together on a single aircraft project. In the United States meanwhile, the efforts toward SST projects gradually narrowed to one, the Boeing 2707, an aircraft whose schedule lagged behind its rivals', and which was ultimately cancelled before it flew.

In the Soviet Union, the SST program was placed in the hands of the Tupolev design bureau, an entity with a great deal of large aircraft experience. The mandate was to prevent the West from having an SST monopoly. Whatever can be said about Soviet

Below and opposite: The Tu-144 No 77102 at Paris in 1973 shortly before it crashed.

Above: Number 77102, with its nose drooped for subsonic flight, on landing approach. *Facing page top:* Number 77102 prior to the 3 June 1973 crash at the Paris Air Show. *Facing page bottom:* Number 77144 was perhaps the first of series production Tu-144s.

Premier Nikita Khruschev, it can certainly be added that he was a true nationalist, a man who wanted to overcome his peoples' collective inferiority complex through spectacular technological triumphs. He had done it once with the first satellite in orbit (1957), and he had done it again with the first man in space (1961). Next, he intended to see the Soviet Union be the first to field a team of SSTs on the world's commercial air routes. If British Airways, Air France and Pan American were planning SSTs, then there was simply no question of the Soviet state airline Aeroflot also having SSTs.

The development of the Tupolev Tu-144 directly parallelled that of the Anglo-French Concorde project, and no doubt benefitted greatly from public discussion of the Concorde's design evolution. In fact, the Tu-144 was referred to in the Western press as 'Concordeski.'

The Tu-144 prototype was 194 feet 11 inches long (nine feet shorter than the Concorde), with a wing span of 90 feet 9 inches (seven feet greater than the Concorde), although the production types would be 215.5 feet long, with a wing span of 94.5 feet. The gross weight of the Tu-144 was 397,000 pounds, compared to 408,000 pounds for the Concorde. The Tu-144 was designed to carry up to 126 passengers, while the Concorde had a capacity of 144. Each was designed to cruise at more than twice the speed of sound.

The Tu-144 became the first SST to fly, on 31 December 1968 with Eduard Elyan and Mikhail Kozlov at the controls. The Concorde made its debut just two months later. The larger, 350-passenger Boeing 2707 was scrapped two years later without having flown. The Tu-144's first flight was reportedly the result of a desperate, almost panicked race to not only beat the Concorde, but to squeeze out at least one flight before the end of the year. For both aircraft, however, the process of getting into airline service would take many trying years.

The Concorde entered service with both British Airways and Air France on 21 January 1976, nine years after the first flight. Because of noise and environmental concerns, and because of the oil crisis of 1974, international sales to over a dozen countries that had expressed interest evaporated, and these two companies were the only ones to buy Concordes, although several other airlines, such as Delta and Singapore, used them briefly under lease arrangements. Just nine aircraft were completed, and they were tried on a number of routes. At first, the Concorde failed to demonstrate any commercial viability. However, it ultimately proved its worth on the highly travelled, and

lucrative, North Atlantic route connecting London and Paris with New York and Washington.

The second prototype Tu-144, meanwhile, had just been proudly debuted at the 1973 Paris Air Show, when it disintegrated in mid-air before the horrified onlookers, killing its flight crew. Plans to put Tu-144s into service between Moscow and various Western capitals were cancelled and an embarrassed Aeroflot began to pick up the pieces. The Tu-144 had been intended to fly as the standard-bearer of a new era in Soviet commercial aviation. She was to have been to the 1970s what the *Maksim Gorkii* was supposed to have been to the 1930s, a demonstration to the world of the power and glory of Soviet technology. Yet when Aeroflot finally put her into service in December 1975, she was trucking freight between Moscow and Alma Ata.

She hauled cargo to the Far East for nearly two years before Aeroflot decided to take a chance with scheduled passenger flights, and even then, the Tu-144 was used only on domestic flights, and was unable to fly for five of the first six scheduled flights. The Tu-144s carried passengers for only seven months when a fatal crash caused Aeroflot to take them off the schedule entirely in June 1978.

The Tu-144s were again relegated to freight service and, although there were reports of a much-improved Tu-144D in 1979, the last Tu-144 was probably unceremoniously mothballed in the early 1980s. The Tu-144 was an example of an airplane that was trusted by no one, not even by its supporters. The Concorde had been a costly white elephant in her early years, but she flew her schedule, found her niche and finally paid off. The Tu-144 had been pushed so fast and so hard that she reached service with more inherent flaws than her makers could correct. Aeroflot had desperately wanted the Tu-144, but the Tu-144 had let them down.

Below and facing page: The production series Tu-144s, first placed in service in 1975, were 20 feet longer than the prototypes.

TWO WHO MIGHT HAVE BEEN AMONG THE BEST AND ONE WHO MAY YET BE

The Douglas Super DC-3

The Douglas DC-3 first flew on 17 December 1935, the thirty-second anniversary of the Wright Brothers' flight at Kitty Hawk. In many ways it was just as momentous of an occasion. The DC-3 single-handedly revolutionized commercial air transportation. Compared to what had gone before, the DC-3 was worlds apart. The DC-3 was quiet, reliable, comfortable, economical, fast and safe. Within two years it was the standard and foremost airliner in the world, and was in service with most of the world's airlines. During World War II, the military versions—C-47, C-53, R4D and Dakota—proved themselves in every corner of the globe. Indeed, more than five decades after they first flew, dozens of Douglas DC-3s are *still* in service around the world.

You might call the DC-3 the greatest airplane that ever flew, and you'd get little argument and find almost no one who'd rank it below third. Having said all this, it seems preposterous that an

airplane called Super DC-3 would make anyone's 'worst' list, but therein lies a tale.

The DC-3 had been in the crest of its spectacular prime when World War II happened. Suddenly there was no more world market for airliners. When the war ended in 1945, a great deal had happened in the world of aviation technology. Douglas Aircraft of Santa Monica, California had what was once the world's foremost airliner, an aircraft whose reputation was nothing short of legendary, but competitors like Martin and Convair had now developed faster, newer and more economical twin-engined airliners—airplanes with such innovations as tricycle landing gear—to feed into the market. Quite simply, the DC-3 was now outdated! It was simply no longer at the leading edge of airliner technology.

At the same time, Douglas realized that there was a vast world market for the DC-3 on secondary and tertiary air routes, but

Below: The first Super DC-3, with its new engines and tall tail, was first flown in 1949, 14 years after the original DC-3. An extensive sales tour failed to sell more than three of the new airplanes. The market had changed dramatically.

there were also thousands of very inexpensive military surplus C-47s and Dakotas on the market to meet the need.

Douglas sought to address the situation with what seemed at the time to be an obvious solution—the Super DC-3. The prototype that rolled out in the spring of 1949 had a wingspan of 94 feet 6 inches, and was 67 feet 9 inches long, three feet longer than the original. This translated into a 40-passenger capacity, which was a 30 percent improvement over the original. The tail, similar to that of the new Douglas DC-6, was a foot taller. The engines were Wright R-1820 radials, delivering 1475 hp, 275 hp better than the engines on the original DC-3.

Donald Douglas, Jr, the son of the company's founder and president, immediately undertook a 10,000-mile publicity tour to promote the new aircraft. During the course of his demonstrations, he found that almost everyone *loved* the Super DC-3. Many of the airlines and pilots that gave it a try had known and loved the original DC-3, and they found Super DC-3 to be everything it had been and more. It had more passenger capacity, more range and more power.

From what was being said publicly, Douglas was predicting orders for at least 60 Super DC-3s. However, when the dust from the promotional tour had settled, and the ink had dried on the actual sales contracts, Douglas had sold exactly *three* Super DC-3s, all to Capital Airlines. No one else wanted to commit to an updated 1935 design, when there were plenty of high-40s designs on the market.

Capital received its first Super DC-3 in July 1950, and a year later, Douglas sold the original Super DC-3 to the US Air Force under the designation YC-129. Eventually, the US Navy bought the YC-129 and gave Douglas a contract to upgrade 100 of its existing DC-3s (Navy designation R4D) to Super DC-3 standard.

On the commercial side, however, Douglas had completely and utterly misjudged the market. There would be no further sales of the new planes to any other airlines. It was simply a matter of cost. The unit cost of the Super DC-3 was $200,000 at a time when a great many surplus DC-3s were on the market for $8000. The Super DC-3 was better than the original, but it was far from being 25 times better, and in the marketplace it was probably 25 times worse, a monument to the folly of nostalgia.

Below: The US Navy helped save the Super DC-3 program by commissioning Douglas to upgrade 100 of its DC-3s (Navy designation R4D) to Super DC-3 standard under the designation R4D-8.

The Northrop F-20 Tigershark

It was a story very much like that of the Douglas Super DC-3. The idea was to take an existing airplane with a spectacular track record, improve it and market the updated version. The only problem in both cases was that the airplane in question was so completely associated with an earlier era that the new version—despite wonderful, far reaching improvements, was cursed with the stigma of being a has-been. The Super DC-3 survived because of US Navy contracts, but failed in the commercial marketplace. Northrop, on the other hand, failed to sell a single Tigershark to anyone.

Born in 1980, the F-20 was a follow-on to Northrop's highly successful F-5 Tiger, one of the most versatile and widely used workhorse jet fighters in history. Originally designated F-5G, the Tigershark was redesignated in US Air Force nomenclature when Northrop made the convincing argument that it really *was* new enough to justify a new designation. The F-20 was a highly-touted, low-cost fighter aircraft which *should* have been to the 1980s and 1990s, what the F-5 had been to the 1960s.

The Tigershark impressed nearly every pilot that flew it—the great Chuck Yeager included—and it impressed every accountant that compared it to any similar, competitive aircraft. For the price, it was the best airplane of its type in the world. Northrop even went so far as to embark on a multi-million dollar advertising campaign—including buying full page ads throughout the aviation press—to insure that the F-20 was not only the best, but the most successful.

This effort went on for years, with countless demonstrations, sales trips and interested potential buyers. Three demonstrators were built at company expense, and they logged a total of 1543 flights between 1982 and 1986. The F-20 could go from a cold start to an altitude of 32,000 feet in 90 seconds in any weather. It could fly 2000 miles without refueling, and it could fly at twice the speed of sound. It could fly half again more missions than its nearest competitor in the same amount of time. It met or bettered all planned performance and reliability objectives—and it was inexpensive to buy and to operate.

The F-20 was the plane that was too good to fail, but in the end, not a single Tigershark was ever sold. The F-20 was cursed by its similarity to the older F-5. Third World countries that should have wanted it for budgetary reasons simply wanted newer—albeit more expensive—aircraft for reasons of prestige. It also didn't help that two out of the three demonstrators crashed over the years, but those losses were not directly attributable to the airplane.

The last straw came in November 1986. Several nations had suggested that they would take the F-20 if the US Air Force selected it as their new 'low-cost air defense fighter.' The choice for the Air Force was between the F-20 and the General Dynamics F-16. Choosing the F-20 for this new role would mean having to also develop a supply and maintenance organization to support it. They already had adopted the F-16 for other tasks, so the logistical support was already in place. The Air Force picked the F-16.

Having spent $1.2 billion of its own money to develop the Tigershark, Northrop decided to cut its losses and cancel the whole program. The single remaining prototype continues to be rented out for television commercials and may one day be donated to a museum, where she will sit as a monument to the genius that created her and the dogged determination that tried and failed to sell her. The Tigershark may well have been the best fighter of her era on most accounts, but she was cursed with having been the right plane at such an incredibly *wrong* time.

Below: Northrop advertising accurately extolled the virtues of an exceptional warplane. During 1985 and 1986, Northrop expended a great deal of money in the climax of the company's efforts to sell the F-20 Tigershark.

Ultimately this fine aircraft was not so much a victim of its own shortcomings—which were nil—but a victim of circumstance. The Tigershark was the right plane, but the timing was not.

After the cancellation of the Tigershark program in 1986, Northrop continued to build F-5s for over two years, while the single surviving F-20 prototype was rented out to advertising agencies for use as a flying and non-flying backdrop in television commercials for automobiles, sparkplugs and, in 1989, flashlights!

The Northrop B-2 Stealth Bomber

With a price tag of $532 million that makes her literally worth her weight in gold, the B-2 became the airplane that everybody—from the US Congress to the American media—loves to hate. As this book goes to press, the B-2 hasn't been around long enough to prove whether she deserves to be placed in a list of history's worst aircraft. Indeed, from what we know, the B-2 itself will probably be a major milestone in the history of aviation. What has been demonstrated is that the B-2 *program* is so costly and vulnerable that bad publicity came close to actually killing the airplane. It wasn't the first time this had happened with a big ticket airplane. The cost of the Rockwell International B-1 made it a political football in the mid-1970s and would end up making it about a decade too late and a good deal more costly than it should have been, but with the B-2 there is a price tag so steep that it makes even the most pro-defense congressmen uneasy.

The B-2 was conceived in mystery and born into controversy. She spent the decade of the 1980s lurking in her secret lair. She was like a mythical beast, well-known, but never seen—the stuff of legends. An airplane that was invisible on radar. She was ethereal and magic.

From the time she was first mentioned in public during the 1980 presidential campaign, she had a mystique that went far beyond any facts that we knew about her. If it hadn't been for the fact that President Jimmy Carter desperately needed a weapons system to hang his hat on, she might have remained secret for another decade.

Carter had come to office in 1976, during an era when—because of the Vietnam War—the American electorate was sick

Facing page: Jack Northrop's unorthodox YB-35 Flying Wing of 1949 evolved ultimately to the B-2—seen *below* on its first takeoff—four decades later.

of everything military. He had promised to cancel the Rockwell B-1 program and he did. By 1980, times had changed. The United States was beginning to pay the price for the years of neglecting its defense establishment. Carter was running an uphill election battle against Ronald Reagan, who promised to rebuild America's once-proud military might.

Jimmy Carter had an ace in the hole, however. He knew that the Air Force was secretly developing a revolutionary type of strategic bomber that employed a basket of technologies known as 'stealth' that would make it virtually invisible to enemy radar. He decided, in August 1980, to let Defense Secretary Harold Brown leak just enough information about this 'stealth bomber' to make Carter appear to the public as one who quietly and secretly 'cared' about defense. Carter's ploy failed to get him elected, but it gave aviation enthusiasts and Soviet spies their first tantalizing inkling of the aircraft that would be 'the mystery plane of the decade.'

The Reagan Administration brought down the veil of secrecy upon the 'stealth bomber' project, and little more was known for years. By 1985 we had learned that the prime contractor for the mystery ship was Northrop, and this, in turn, led to speculation that the new airplane would have a 'flying wing' configuration, because Northrop's only other heavy bombers had been the YB-35 and YB-49 Flying Wings of the early 1950s. We also learned that when President Reagan revived the B-1 program, there was a behind-closed-doors debate over whether to try to

bring 'stealth' on line sooner to obviate the need for the B-1. Nevertheless, the 'stealth bomber' remained a mystery, referred to by the US Air Force simply as the Advanced Technology Bomber (ATB).

When the B-2 was finally rolled out in November 1988, it was the most heavily restricted *public* rollout in history. Indeed, there was a public rollout only because the Air Force decided that it would be impossible to flight test so large an aircraft in total secrecy. Only 500 guests were on hand, and armed guards with German Shepherds outnumbered reporters by a ratio of four to one. Nobody was allowed to look behind the B-2.

The B-2 is a huge, tailless bat of an airplane with a wingspan of 172 feet—greater than that of the B-1B, and almost as great as the B-52. Because it is a 'flying wing' like Northrop's YB-35 and YB-49 of the 1940s, it has no fuselage and, as such, is only 69 feet long. It is powered by four General Electric F-118-GE-100 turbofans, each of which can deliver 19,000 pounds of thrust. Its precise weapons-carrying capability is unknown, but it is probably no greater than the B-1B, and, like the B-1B, the entire payload is carried in an internal bomb bay, which contains a rotary launcher capable of being configured with Air Launched Cruise Missiles (ALCM), Short Range Attack Missiles (SRAM), or a choice of conventional or nuclear bombs.

When everything is said and done, however, the most unique and important feature of the B-2—indeed its entire purpose for being—is its stealth technology. Stealth is, in fact, a whole

basket of technologies designed to make the airplane virtually invisible to radar. These include contours and surfaces that absorb rather than reflect radar waves, thus giving the B-2 the radar signature more characteristic of a bird than a B-52.

In fact, the B-2 and its development technology may one day be vindicated, but in her early days the B-2 has had a tough burden to bear. In its report on the November 1988 rollout, *Time* magazine decided that the B-2 was a bomber that the United States 'cannot afford.' In its 10 July 1989 issue, the newsmagazine *US News & World Report* named the B-2 to head its list of America's 'Worst Weapons.' It was this 'tribute' that made us decide to consider the B-2 in these pages.

Ironically, Northrop and the US Air Force chose 10 July 1989 to initiate the B-2's taxi tests, and the first flight came on 17 July with Northrop B-2 chief test pilot Bruce Hinds and Air Force Colonel Richard Couch in the cockpit. Much to the chagrin of critics, the flight went smoothly and the big bat touched down lightly at Edwards AFB.

However, when the Bush administration announced that the annual procurement cost for the B-2 would be $8 billion, Congressional Armed Services Committee Chairman Les Aspin moaned that 'there are only 12 countries in the world that have defense budgets greater than $8 billion a year. We would be spending more on the B-2 than any Warsaw Pact country spends except Russia and East Germany. Is it conceivable that we are going to do this? No chance!'

Prior to the B-2's first flight, it was widely reported that the unit cost of the B-2 would be $532 million, a figure arrived at by dividing the $70.2 billion program cost by 132 aircraft. However, Northrop pointed out that the total included $22.5 billion that had already been spent on development, and that additional aircraft would cost less than half what was being bantered about in the press. By eliminating training and base construction from the program, the actual unit cost was in the area of $250 million.

Armed with this information, supporters of the B-2 in both the Congress and the Senate headed off attempts to kill the B-2 program entirely, but they did accept delays in procurement that would save money in the near term, but which would, ironically, force the ultimate cost higher by spreading out the time it would take to build 132 B-2s.

The B-2 is ultimately a hostage to her own advanced design. She is the albatross around her own neck. Because she is so far ahead of other aircraft, her cost may well be so high that it will be unaffordable, and therefore she will never be in service long enough to prove conclusively whether she is among the world's best, or among the world's worst.

Below: Seen here banking into the waning rays of the setting sun, the B-2 represents an era so new to aviation history that the perspective by which it can be evaluated simply does not yet exist. Ultimately, the B-2 may be remembered as the airplane that precipitated perestroika in the Soviet Union. If so, it will have ironically obviated its own requirement, and the expense that led to its being considered 'worst' will be considered worthwhile and unnecessary in the same breath.

Index

PHOTO CREDITS